D0071612

Proper Form, Pure and Simple

# Proper Form, Pure and Simple

## A Handbook for English Grammar

HORACE (SKIP) ROBINSON

RESOURCE *Publications* · Eugene, Oregon

PROPER FORM, PURE AND SIMPLE
A Handbook for English Grammar

Copyright © 2012 Horace Robinson. All rights reserved. Except for brief quotations in critical publications or reviews, no part of this book may be reproduced in any manner without prior written permission from the publisher. Write: Permissions, Wipf and Stock Publishers, 199 W. 8th Ave., Suite 3, Eugene, OR 97401.

Resource Publications
An Imprint of Wipf and Stock Publishers
199 W. 8th Ave., Suite 3
Eugene, OR 97401

www.wipfandstock.com

ISBN 13: 978-1-61097-183-6

Manufactured in the U.S.A.

To my wife, Wilma, for her patience and encouragement during the decade-long quest to draft an English book that could be understood

To the three thousand students of Southeastern Oklahoma State University who served as the proving ground for *Proper Form, Pure and Simple*

To my colleagues, administrators, and higher education officials who championed the writing of this handbook

# Contents

# List of Tables

# Preface

This handbook is not for the scholar, nor is it intended to address every grammatical issue that could arise in the study of the English language. It is crafted and directed toward the intelligent learner or on-the-job professional who got off on the wrong foot in his/her pursuit of proper form. Reasons for the poor start are many and varied, including non-interest in learning, trauma during the instructional period, and to be realistic, ineffective instruction.

During my teaching of forty classes of English 1113, it dawned upon me that the examples which were clear to me were not always clear to the students. Many high-sounding, melodious definitions were indicative of where the professor was and not where the students were. This realization should have been axiomatic, "Accept the students where they are and begin at the very beginning."

As a result, the learner or the on-the-job professional is the target audience of this commentary. These two groups are the determining factors in the wording of any illustration, example or definition. (All words pertaining to Proper Form have been capitalized to indicate their importance and specificity and to increase the simplicity of the handbook.) The major issues of where the student is intellectually, how to move him/her to the next level of understanding, and how best to affirm the learner as he/she progresses, have been foremost in determining what should be included in this handbook.

The goal of this small missile is to enhance the careers of capable young people who, for one valid reason or another, missed this vital element of their education. It is designed to replace complexity with simplicity and to reduce verbosity to succinctness. This will allow the student or professional worker to leave guesswork and mind games behind and to put the language together with skill and confidence.

—Horace (Skip) Robinson,
November, 2011

# Acknowledgments

In academic pursuits, few projects are accomplished alone. The following contributors have enthusiastically shared their knowledge, their creativity, and their encouragement to bring *Proper Form, Pure and Simple* to our readers.

Dr. C. Henry Gold—for the high value he places on proper form and for his unceasing excitement for the project

Mrs. Stacia Harrison—for her skill and perseverance in manuscript production

Mrs. Betty Clay—for the unselfish application of her talents in the design of the thirty Tables that are included in this handbook

Mrs. Jackye Gold—for her experience in teaching proper form and for her expertise as a copy editor

Dr. Wilma Shires—for her knowledge of proper form and for her willingness to share that knowledge

# Introduction

Let's visit! Many of you who are reading this little handbook are hiding a deep, dark secret. You do not know Proper English Form. This does not mean that you are deficient in any way. It simply means that you have not learned Proper Form to this point. The faint of heart may be saying, "I try, but I just can't learn it." Oh! Yes, you can.

Has a teacher ever started at the beginning with you, at the very beginning? I remember with painful clarity being in your shoes, but I also remember a professor who was willing to start at the very beginning in her teaching of Proper Form.

Learning Proper Form is much like building a house; you need to understand basic definitions. One summer, my son and I were attempting to build a lake house. Neither of us is a builder; he is a computer design technician; and I, an English professor. We envisioned a beautiful interior curved staircase, but it was beyond our skill level. A seventy-year-old man was hired to build the complex staircase, and my son and I were left to handle the simple, straight, outdoor staircase to the porch. Noticing our hesitancy to take on the allegedly simple task, the old fellow leaned over the porch rail and said, "You can git them 2x6's out of the scrap pile over there and cut 'em with the chop saw, the table saw or the Saws All if ye want to—but rip 'em on three feet, then cut your risers on thirty-seven degrees, and ye got her done." Problem: what is a chop saw and a Saws All? What is the thirty-seven degrees all about?

Mr. Grubbs did not begin at the beginning. He assumed we knew some basic definitions when we had no idea of what these strange-sounding names meant. This made my son and me, two reasonably intelligent men, feel and look inadequate. I want to spare you this feeling of inadequacy or perhaps rescue some of you from this feeling of inadequacy that overwhelms you when it comes to using Proper Form. Let's begin at the very beginning and take slow, sure, steps together. All right?

## Beginning Again

Before you can learn Proper Form, you must deal with the grammatical debris that spins like a tornado above your head. Since you have never understood Proper Form, you most likely have concocted various ways to beat the system. Probably, in the early grades, you learned to "guess" which form was correct. And as you matured, you created make-believe tests to determine which form was correct. These tests were usually based on what "sounded right" as opposed to the true test of rule.

And then it happened! With your mind awhirl, employing your guessing games and trusting what "sounded right" to determine correctness, you ran into the mother of all English teachers, the dreaded Mrs. McGuillacuddy. Chop saws and Saws Alls are simple compared to the stream of terms that flowed effortlessly from her lips. She joyfully hurled her Gerunds, Appositives, Participles, Subjunctive Moods, and Comparative Degrees into the mix, and these terms were added to that swirling, irrelevant mass above your head.

It may be your first day on the job or your first assignment in Freshman English, or the first time your employer says, "Please write a narrative about the history of our company since 1990." But sooner or later the grammatical debris (unsuccessful English comprehension) that has swirled above your head for so long will collapse upon you, threatening your very life in the academic or business world.

Is this where you are? Are you under what feels like tons and tons of unsuccessful English lessons? If so, do not feel defeated or incapable of freeing yourself from the debris which has collapsed upon you. You can crawl from under the debris that covers you! You can separate it, analyze it, and identify the parts which now swirl unrelated and undefined in your mind. Once these things are done, the complexity of Proper Form will be cut in half. So, let's go to work; separating, analyzing, and identifying your grammatical debris.

# Chapter 1

## Parts of Speech versus Parts of a Sentence

First, let's separate the Parts of Speech (eight of them) from the Parts of a Sentence. Right now, in your mind, they probably exist in one, big, meaningless pile. Let's see how Parts of Speech differ from the Parts of a Sentence.

- The *Parts of Speech* could be thought of as the *raw material* from which a Sentence is made. They are the following:

  1. NOUN
  2. PRONOUN
  3. VERB
  4. ADJECTIVE
  5. ADVERB
  6. PREPOSITION
  7. CONJUNCTION
  8. INTERJECTION

If you were building a house, the lumber company would drop a load of lumber (raw material) at your building site. In the raw material pile would be various sizes of lumber: 2x4's, 2x6's, 1x12's, 2x8's, and so forth. These are the raw materials from which your house will be constructed. In the same way, the Parts of Speech (Nouns, Pronouns, Verbs, Adjectives, Adverbs, Prepositions, Conjunctions and Interjections) are the raw materials from which you will build your Sentences.

- *The Parts of a Sentence*, on the other hand, could be thought of as the *new names* given to the raw materials once they are placed in the Sentence and have a given function. Some of these *Sentence Parts* are the following:

1. SUBJECT
2. PREDICATE
3. DIRECT OBJECT
4. INDIRECT OBJECT
5. OBJECT OF A PREPOSITION

Now, don't panic or let your mind go blank just because you have seen the debris spread before you and have heard familiar terms which you have never understood. Instead, let's continue with the building analogy. In building a house, you would go to the woodpile and get lumber. The boards would be called 2x4's, 2x6's, 1x12's, 2x8's, and so forth. But once these boards are put into the structure of your house and assume a *given function*, their names change according to what function they serve. The 2x4, when it *functions* as a wall support is called by its new name, a stud. The 2x6, when it *functions* as a window support is called a header. The 2x8, when it *functions* as a flooring support is called by its new name, a joist. In the same way, when you take the Parts of Speech (raw materials) and place them into a structure called a *Sentence*, they get new names according to how they *function* in that Sentence. Their new names (Sentence Parts) are, as listed above, Subject, Predicate, Direct Object, Indirect Object, Object of a Preposition, and others which lie beyond the scope of this handbook.

Now we are getting somewhere! You understand the principle. What you need now is a simple, specific example to prove to yourself that you know the difference between the *Parts of Speech* and the *Parts of a Sentence*. (In future chapters, I will define each of the Parts of Speech as well as many of the Sentence Parts in simple terms.) For now, please accept the definition in parenthesis as you continue reasoning.

In understanding the difference between a *Part of Speech* (raw material) and a *Part of a Sentence*, consider the word "boy" in the following Sentences:

- The *boy* hit the ball.

  As a *Part of Speech* (raw material), "boy" is a Noun (name of a person, place, or thing).

- The *boy* hit the ball.

  As a *Part of a Sentence*, "boy" is the Subject (the topic of the Sentence). You see, the Noun receives a new name according to how it functions in the Sentence.

Do you see how "boy" is a Noun in the raw material pile, but once it is placed into the structure of a Sentence and assumes a given function, it gets a new name, Subject? Good job!

If you have doubts, reread the information, slowly, from beginning to end. There's no need to spend the rest of your life guessing, depending upon unreliable tests of sound, and smothering under tons and tons of grammatical debris.

Now, let's briefly define the Eight Parts of Speech.

The Eight Parts of Speech are the raw material from which a Sentence is made.

1. Noun: the name of a person, place or thing

   John Smith: Person
   Denver, Colorado: Place
   Tree: Thing
   Common Noun: street
   Proper Noun: Elm Street

2. Verb: a word that shows action or state of being

   Example: jump, run, sing, smile, play, dance, (be)
   Jack jumped with joy.  Jumped is a Verb as a Part of Speech (raw material pile).
   Jack jumped with joy.  Jumped is a Predicate as a *Sentence Part*.

3. Pronoun: a word used in place of a Noun

   John Jones: Noun       Katy: Noun       Gift: Noun
   He:          Pronoun   She:  Pronoun   It:   Pronoun

4. Adjective: a word that modifies (describes) a Noun by telling which one, what kind, or how many

> A spotted pony = an Adjective telling which one.
> A bright day = an Adjective telling what kind.
> Seven fish = an Adjective telling how many.

Pony is a Noun; "spotted" describes it. (Tells "which one")
Day is a Noun; "bright" describes it. (Tells "what kind")
Fish is a Noun; "seven" describes it. (Tells "how many")

You've just learned, once and for all, that *Adjectives describe Nouns.*

5. Adverb: a word that modifies (describes) a Verb (action word) by telling how, when, or where

> The child played happily. (An Adverb telling how)
> He bathes daily. (An Adverb telling when)
> He climbed *high* in the tree. (An Adverb telling where)

Played is a Verb; "happily" describes it. (Tells "how")
Bathe is a Verb; "daily" describes it. (Tells "when")
Climbed is a Verb; "high" describes it. (Tells "where")

You have just learned, once and for all, that *Adverbs describe Verbs.*

6. Preposition: a word that shows the relationship between a Noun and another word in a Sentence

> The border of Oklahoma is crooked.

(See how "of" shows the relationship between border and Oklahoma?)

> We hauled hay by moonlight.

(See how "by" shows the relationship between moonlight and hauled?)

> How much is that doggie in the window?

(See how "in" shows the relationship between window and doggie?)

You have just learned that a *Preposition shows relationships. It is a connector.* Sometimes it is called a weak connector because it can connect Words and Phrases only.

7. Conjunction: a word that can connect Words, Phrases, and Clauses (a group of words that has a Subject and Predicate)

(A Conjunction can connect Words.) The men and women worked hard.

See how "and" connects the Words men and women?

(A Conjunction can connect Phrases.) It was either a raccoon or a fat, bushy-tailed cat.

See how "or" connects raccoon and the phrase "a fat, bushy-tailed cat"?

(A Conjunction can connect Clauses.) Police surveillance doubled when crime increased.

See how "when" connects surveillance with the Clause "crime increased"?

Like a Preposition, a Conjunction is also a connector. Sometimes the conjunction is called a strong connector because it can connect Words, Phrases, and *Clauses.* This is as far as you need to go for now; there will be more about Conjunctions in Chapter VI.


8. Interjection: a word that shows strong feeling

> *Help!* I am bleeding.
> *No!* Do not touch.
> *Wow!* What a sunset.

The definitions of the Eight Parts of Speech are a must for understanding Proper Form. You may have a hard time taking them seriously because you have heard them before, and you think you know what they mean. Take "Noun" for example. You understand Noun until you are told that a Gerund can be used any way a Noun can be used. A Gerund is half Verb and half Noun. And then what if you were asked to make a Sentence using a Gerund? (This would be hard because you simply did not grasp the general definition of a Noun as a *Part of Speech.*) It may be wise to go back over the definitions one more time. It will take some effort, but you are pouring a strong foundation on which to build an unshakable "Proper Form" structure.

Now let's talk about the other half of the equation, *Parts of a Sentence.* Remember, when a Part of Speech is placed into a Sentence, it becomes a *Sentence Part.* Then, it gets a new name according to how it functions. Below are the definitions of some of these Sentence Parts (new names):

- Subject: the topic of the Sentence (or, colloquially, what the Sentence is about)
- Predicate: the action word in the Sentence
- Direct Object: receives the action of the Predicate (action word)
- Indirect Object: to whom or for whom something is done
- Object of a Preposition: a Noun (or Pronoun) connected to the Sentence by a Preposition

The difference between *Parts of Speech* and *Parts of a Sentence* can be seen easily as we walk through some Sentences together. Watch these closely!

| | |
|---|---|
| The *girl* sang a solo. | "Girl" is a Noun as a *Part of Speech*. (Raw material pile) "Girl" is the Subject as a *Sentence Part*. Go back and read the definition of a Subject. |
| The ball hit the *boy*. | "Boy" is a Noun as a *Part of Speech*. (Raw material pile) <br><br> "Boy" is a Direct Object as a Sentence Part. Go back and read the definition of a Direct Object. A simple way to recognize a Direct Object is to find the Predicate and ask "what or whom." If there is an answer, it is the Direct Object. |
| Dad gave the *boy* a ball. | "Boy" is a Noun as a *Part of Speech*. (Raw material pile) <br><br> "Boy" is an Indirect Object as a *Sentence Part*. Go back and read the definition of an Indirect Object. |
| The puppy played with the *boy*. | "Boy" is a Noun as a *Part of Speech*. (Raw material pile) <br><br> "Boy" is an Object of the Preposition (with) as a *Sentence Part*. Go back and read the definition of an Object of a Preposition. |

See the difference between the *Parts of Speech* (eight of them) and the *Parts of a Sentence?*

Now let me click the refresh button and give you a side-by-side comparison of the *Parts of Speech* and the *Parts of a Sentence.*

Table 1. Parts of Speech versus Parts of a Sentence

| *Parts of Speech* | *Parts of a Sentence* |
| :---: | :---: |
| Noun | Subject |
| Pronoun | Predicate |
| Verb | Direct Object |
| Adjective | Indirect Object |
| Adverb | Object of a Preposition |
| Preposition | |
| Conjunction | |
| Interjection | |

## Table 2. Parts of Speech Worksheet

Out of this woodpile (raw materials), identify each Part of Speech.
There are eight Parts of Speech. See Table 1.

| | | |
|---|---|---|
| Boy___N___ | Tree__N___ | Horse_N___ |
| He___P N___ | She_____ | They_____ |
| Run___V___ | Jump_____ | Sing_____ |
| Sweetly___A DV.___ | Always_____ | Weekly_____ |
| Beautiful___ADJ___ | Red_____ | Six_____ |
| Of___P___ | With _____ | Like_____ |
| And___C___ | But _____ | Or _____ |
| Help!___I___ | Oh!_____ | Mercy!_____ |

## Table 3. Answers for Parts of Speech Worksheet

| | | |
|---|---|---|
| Boy Noun | Tree Noun | Horse Noun |
| He Pronoun | She Pronoun | They Pronoun |
| Run Verb | Jump Verb | Sing Verb |
| Sweetly Adverb | Always Adverb | Weekly Adverb |
| Beautiful Adjective | Red Adjective | Six Adjective |
| Of Preposition | With Preposition | Like Preposition |
| And Conjunction | But Conjunction | Or Conjunction |
| Help! Interjection | Oh! Interjection | Mercy! Interjection |

Remember, once a *Part of Speech* (raw material) has been placed into a Sentence, it becomes a *Sentence Part* and gets a new name. Before proceeding, let's review these Sentence Parts (new names) and give your confidence a boost!

Once you are sure that you understand them, you may complete your Parts of a Sentence Worksheet.

REVIEW OF SENTENCE PARTS

- Subject—the topic of the Sentence (or, colloquially, what the Sentence is about)

- Predicate—the action word in the Sentence (Verb in the raw material pile)

- Direct Object—receives the action of the Predicate (ask what or whom)

- Indirect Object—to whom or for whom something is done, said, shown, or given

- Object of a Preposition—a Noun (or Pronoun) connected to the Sentence by a Preposition

Table 4. Parts of a Sentence Worksheet

Mark the underlined words with S for Subject; DO for Direct Object; IO for Indirect Object; OP for Object of a Preposition; P for Predicate.

    S   P        DO      OP
1. John carried the water to the sink.

     S     P     PD     OP
2. The men hauled hay by moonlight.

     S    P     DO       OP
3. The boy combed his hair like his father.

      OP       S   P       oP
4. In the morning, the ducks fly over the pond.

        S    P   IDO     DO
5. The game warden gave them the award.

    S     P   IDO     DO          OP
6. Susan showed James the answer to the algebra problem.

     S   P        OP
7. The squirrel ran behind the tree.

    S  P      IDO    DO    OP
8. He gave the squirrels a drink of water.

     S    P  DO     OP
9. The ball hit him on the arm.

        OP       S     P      DO       oP
10. During the night, the soldiers carried their comrades to safety.

Table 5. Answers for Parts of a Sentence Worksheet

1. S,P,DO,OP

2. S,P,DO,OP

3. S,P,DO,OP

4. OP,S,P,OP

5. S,P,IO,DO

6. S,P,IO,DO,OP

7. S,P,OP

8. S,P,IO,DO,OP

9. S,P,DO,OP

10. OP,S,P,DO,OP

In case you had any problems with the Parts of a Sentence Worksheet, a slow walk through these next five Sentences will solve them for you. Students often say, "I didn't really 'get it' until we had the 'slow walk' exercise." So take your time; walk slowly and thoughtfully through these five Sentences. You are doing well.

Identify the Parts of a Sentence represented by each italicized word.

1. The beautiful *birds* flew over the house.

    "Birds" is the Subject as a *Sentence Part*. It is the topic of the Sentence, or colloquially, what the Sentence is about.

2. Johnny scared the *birds*.

    "Birds" is the Direct Object as a *Sentence Part*. To identify a Direct Object, find the Predicate and ask, "what or whom." If there is an answer, it is the Direct Object. Johnny scared "what or whom"? He scared the "birds."

3. I'd like to fly with the *birds*.

    "Birds" is the Object of a Preposition as a *Sentence Part*. "With" is a Preposition and "birds" is the Noun that follows a Preposition. Hence, "birds" is the Object of a Preposition.

4. Dad gave the *birds* a drink of water.

    "Birds" is an Indirect Object as a *Sentence Part*. An Indirect Object tells "to whom or for whom" something is said, done, shown, or given. Just for fun, what would "drink" be as a *Sentence Part*? You are correct. It is the Direct Object.

5. Birds *fly* over the rainbow.

    "Fly" is the Predicate as a *Sentence Part*. It is the action word in the Sentence. (Sometimes the words Verb and Predicate are used interchangeably.)

Now that you understand the *Parts of a Sentence*, you can understand these Three Key Definitions easily. I call them the "Big Three" and understanding them will help you put the language together with confidence.

The Big Three

1. *Sentence*: A group of words that has a Subject and a Predicate and makes complete sense

Example: Mother cooked roast for supper.

See the Subject? "Mother"; see the Predicate? "Cooked"? Does it make complete sense? Yes! *It is a Sentence.*

2. *Clause*: A group of words that has a Subject and Predicate—sometimes it makes sense; sometimes it doesn't.

Example: When the ice cracked, the car fell through.

There are two Clauses in this Sentence. See them? One makes sense; the other doesn't. "When the ice cracked"—doesn't make sense. It's called a *Dependent Clause* because it depends on the other Clause for its meaning.

"The car fell through"—makes sense. It's called an *Independent Clause* because it stands alone, and in fact, would make a complete Sentence. *These are Clauses.*

3. *Phrase*: A group of words that has neither Subject nor Predicate and does not make sense

Example: With a puff of smoke…

Consider the group of words, "With a puff of smoke." It has neither Subject nor Predicate and it does not make sense. *It is a Phrase.*

Example: Wagging his long, green, slimy tail…

Consider the group of words, "Wagging his long, green, slimy tail." It has neither Subject nor Predicate and it does not make sense. *It is a Phrase.*

# Chapter 2

## Focusing on Nouns

As promised, let's go back through the *Eight Parts of Speech* and learn about each in detail. At this point, it is tempting to say, "I know all that, so let's get on with the heavy stuff, choosing the right form of Pronoun, and so forth." Choosing the right form of Pronoun can be done any time, after all that's where you learned to *guess*. It is a hundred times more important to learn the *process* rather than the "right answer" at this point. When you learn process, the answers are amazingly simple. Without learning process, it is an endless game of guesswork based on that fickle rule (subjective one) of "what sounds right." Let's learn more about Nouns! All right?

1. A Noun in the raw material pile (Parts of Speech) can become a Subject as a Sentence Part.

   The *boy* hit the ball. (The Subject is "boy"; the topic of the Sentence.)

2. A Noun in the raw material pile (Parts of Speech) can become a Direct Object as a Sentence Part.

   The boy hit the *ball*. (The Direct Object is "ball"; it receives the action of the Predicate.) Remember, you can always find the Direct Object by finding the Predicate and asking the question "what" or "whom." The boy hit (what?) the ball. "Ball" is the Direct Object.

3. A Noun in the raw material pile (Parts of Speech) can become an Object of a Preposition as a Sentence Part.

The boy hit the ball *with* a bat. (The Object of the Preposition is "bat"; "with" is the Preposition.) An Object of a Preposition is a Noun that is connected to the Sentence by a Preposition.

4. A Noun in the raw material pile (Parts of Speech) can become an Indirect Object as a Sentence Part.

John gave *Janey* a ring. (Janey is the Indirect Object, which is to whom or for whom something is done, said, shown, or given.)

Just for fun, let's analyze that last Sentence by giving the Sentence Part (function) of each Noun.

John gave Janey a ring.

John is the Subject; ring is the Direct Object; Janey is the Indirect Object; and gave is the Predicate. You did it. Good job!

Now, let's summarize what you have learned about Nouns, namely that Nouns get "new names" when placed into a Sentence. These new names are Subjects, Direct Objects, Objects of Prepositions, and Indirect Objects. These "new names" (Sentence Parts) are determined by how Nouns function once they are placed into a Sentence.

Several years ago, I was asked to teach a course called "Take the Guesswork out of Grammar" to a group of bi-vocational ministers. Several of them were construction workers and carpenters. When we came to the part of the course that discussed how Parts of Speech (raw material pile) when placed into a Sentence got new names (Parts of a Sentence), I had a great idea for a visual. The group was asked to build a small house and bring it to class, along with some of the raw materials from which the house was constructed. I envisioned a small doll house with several splinters of wood which would serve as the raw material pile. This would make a great, concrete example of the difference between the Parts of Speech and the Parts of a Sentence. I could see myself taking a small splinter of wood from the raw material pile, placing it into the structure of the doll house and saying, "This 2x4 is no longer just a board; it functions as a wall support and its new name is a stud." The students did their homework. At class time, they were prepared with the "house." It took four of them to tilt the house sideways and carry it through the doorway. The raw materials they brought were actual 2x4's. After class, they loaded it into my pickup, and I proudly hauled it home, where it served as a posh dog house for a decade.

# Chapter 3

## Focusing on Pronouns

A Pronoun is a word that is used in the place of a Noun. I will discuss seven types of Pronouns. By using the one-step-at-a-time strategy, you'll be amazed at how quickly you understand Pronouns.

The first one is the *Personal Pronoun*. By definition, it is simply a Pronoun that takes the place of a person.

Stan = Noun.

He = Personal Pronoun.

See how "he" takes the place of Stan? "I get this," you might say, "but what about 'him' and 'her'? Aren't they also Personal Pronouns?" You are correct. Good thinking! "You" and "they" are also Personal Pronouns. Now you've discovered why Pronouns are challenging and why students and on-the-job professionals are tempted to guess at which Pronoun Form is correct.

Pronouns are challenging because they have different forms. To simplify this multi-form complexity, Pronouns are placed into groups, called *Cases*. Do not let the word "Cases" scare you, nor let them become additional pieces of floating debris. (After all, that's how you got under this blanket of meaningless terminology.) Remember the promise you made to yourself, "I'm going to begin at the beginning and embrace the one-step-at-a-time strategy." Oh! You didn't make that promise? Well, make it now, before it's too late!

There are three *Cases* or "groupings" of Pronouns.

| Nominative Case | Objective Case | Possessive Case |
|---|---|---|
| (For Subjects) | (For Objects) | (For Ownership) |
| I | Me | My |

When the Pronoun is a Subject; Use the Nominative Case.

*I* hit the ball. (Not, Me hit the ball.)

When the Pronoun is an Object; Use the Objective Case.

The ball hit *me*. (Not, The ball hit I.)

When the Pronoun shows ownership; Use the Possessive Case.

This is *my* ball. (Not, This is me ball.)

The Pronouns used so far are called 1st Person Pronouns because they represent the *person speaking*. (I = person speaking.) Some Pronouns are called 2nd Person Pronouns because they represent the *person spoken to*. (You = person spoken to.) Other Pronouns are called 3rd Person Pronouns because they represent the *person spoken about*. (He/she/it = person spoken about.) A simple paradigm will clarify this for you.

Table 6. Personal Pronoun Paradigm

| Personal Pronouns | Nominative Case For: Subjects and Predicate Pronouns | | Objective Case For: Direct Objects, Indirect Objects, and Objects of a Preposition. | | Possessive Case For: Showing ownership; Used before a Gerund. | |
|---|---|---|---|---|---|---|
| | Singular | Plural | Singular | Plural | Singular | Plural |
| First Person (speaking) | I | We | Me | Us | My/Mine | Our/Ours |
| Second Person (spoken to) | You | You | You | You | Your/Yours | Your/Yours |
| Third Person (spoken about) | He/She/It | They | Him/Her/It | Them | His/Hers/Its | Their/Theirs |

You see from the paradigm that the pronoun "I" (the person speaking) is singular. "We" (persons speaking) would be plural. "You" (the person spoken to) is singular; "you" (the persons spoken to) would be plural. "He/she/it" (the person spoken about) is singular; "they" (the persons spoken about) would be plural.

You may be thinking at this point, "I can figure some things out for myself, after all I had a 3.5 last semester," or "I am Vice President of my own company." No doubt you are bright, or you wouldn't be studying this. You have great potential, and because of that potential, it is vital that you nail down *Proper Form* once and for all. For those who are not as perceptive as you, there is a plateau awaiting them in their careers from which they can never ascend. So, if you think that this material has been simple thus far, you have kept your end of the bargain, and I have kept mine.

Remember the 1st person is the *person speaking*, as in a first person novel. It will always be, "I climbed the stairs"; "I packed my bag"; "I shut the door"; and so forth. Remember the second person is the person *spoken to*. (You/You) "You climbed the stairs"; "You packed your bag"; "You shut the door"; and so forth. Remember the third person is the person *spoken about*. (He/She/It) "He climbed the stairs"; "He packed his bag"; "He shut the door"; and so forth.

Here is a fail-proof way to deal with the complexity of Pronoun choice. I call it the "Three—Step—Drop." Beginning quarterbacks are usually taught to take three steps backward before throwing a pass. Student athletes understand the necessity of each step, and they attack these complex Pronouns one-step-at-a-time. The "Three—Step—Drop" has been the key to making many a student athlete a grammarian. It will work for you. These three simple steps will allow you to determine the correct Pronoun without guessing and without asking the misleading question, "What sounds right?"

*The Three—Step—Drop:*

1. What is the Sentence Part played by the Pronoun? (Subject, Direct Object, Indirect Object, Object of a Preposition)

2. What Pronoun Case is correct for this Sentence Part? (Nominative, Objective, Possessive) See Table 6.

3. What is the correct Pronoun Form? See Table 6.

If you can answer Step number one, identifying the Sentence Part played by the Pronoun, you have this problem whipped. Steps number two and number three follow logically and easily.

Since identifying the Sentence Part is vital to the "Three—Step—Drop," let's take another look at the definitions of Sentence Parts.

### IDENTIFYING SENTENCE PARTS

Subject—the topic of the Sentence (or, colloquially, what the Sentence is about)

Predicate—the action word in the Sentence (Verb in the raw material pile)

Direct Object—receives the action of the Predicate (ask what or whom)

Indirect Object—to whom or for whom something is done, said, shown, or given

Object of a Preposition—a Noun (or Pronoun) connected to the Sentence by a Preposition

Now, you are ready to put the Three—Step—Drop to the test. Take your time and walk through these Sentences. There is no hurry.

- I/me went fishing.

    Step 1: "I/me" is used as the Subject (the topic of the Sentence).

    Step 2: Subjects require the Nominative Case.

    Step 3: The correct Pronoun form is *I*.

    Consult paradigm, Table 6, if necessary. You probably could have guessed this one, but remember we are learning *process* here and are not trusting the fickle guide of what sounds right.

- Mom called she/her and I/me.

    Step 1: Mom called what or whom? The Pronouns are Direct Objects.

    Step 2: Direct Objects require the Objective Case.

    Step 3: The correct Pronoun forms are *her* and *me*.

- Dad praised Susan and I/me.

    Step 1: Dad praised what or whom? The Pronoun is a Direct Object.

Step 2: Direct Objects require the Objective Case.

Step 3: The proper Pronoun form is *me*. Easy as one, two, three!

- Between you and I/me, the cake is good.

   Step 1: "Between" is a Preposition; hence, the Pronoun is an Object of a Preposition.

   Step 2: Objects of Prepositions require the Objective Case.

   Step 3: The proper Pronoun form is *me*.

   "Between you and I" sounds so cool, but it is so wrong! Excuse me, that last remark must have come right out of a lecture to freshman English students.

- The General gave he/him and I/me an accolade.

   Step 1: The Pronouns are used as Indirect Objects (to whom or for whom something is said, done, shown, or given).

   Step 2: Indirect Objects require the Objective Case.

   Step 3: The proper Pronoun forms are *him* and *me*.

   Just for fun, let's analyze the entire Sentence:

   What Sentence Part is General?_____

   What Sentence Part is gave?_____

   What Sentence Part is accolade?_____

   If you said, "Subject, Predicate, and Direct Object," you are correct.

- The puppy rode with Dad and I/me.

   Step 1: "With" is a Preposition; hence, the Pronoun is used as an Object of a Preposition.

   Step 2: Objects of Prepositions require the Objective Case.

   Step 3: The correct Pronoun form is *me*.

- The professor praised she/her and he/him after the debate.

   Step 1: The Pronouns are used as Direct Objects.

   Step 2: Direct Objects require the Objective Case.

Step 3: The correct Pronoun forms are *her* and *him*.

The remaining Pronouns will respond to this same three-step reasoning process. THE THREE—STEP—DROP WILL WORK ON ALL OF THEM. Now that you understand Pronoun Cases, it will not scare you to look at all seven Pronouns. Take a look at Table 7!

Table 7. Pronoun Paradigm for Types of Pronouns

| | Nominative Case<br>For: Subjects, Predicate Pronouns | Objective Case<br>For: Direct Objects, Indirect Objects, Objects of a Preposition | Possessive Case<br>For: Showing ownership; Used before a Gerund |
|---|---|---|---|
| **Personal Pronouns**<br>First Person<br>Second Person<br>Third Person | **Singular  Plural**<br>I          We<br>You        You<br>He/She/It  They | **Singular  Plural**<br>Me         Us<br>You        You<br>Him/Her/It Them | **Singular  Plural**<br>My/Mine    Our/Ours<br>Your/Yours Your/Yours<br>His/Hers/Its Their/Theirs |
| **Relative Pronouns** | Who<br>Whoever<br>That<br>Which | Whom<br>Whomever<br>That<br>Which | Whose<br>Whosever |
| **Interrogative Pronouns** | Who<br>Whoever<br>Which<br>What | Whom<br>Whomever<br>Which<br>What | Whose<br>Whosever |
| **Reflexive/Intensive Pronouns**<br>First Person<br>Second Person<br>Third Person | | **Singular  Plural**<br>Myself     Ourselves<br>Yourself   Yourselves<br>Himself    Themselves<br>Herself/Itself | |
| **Demonstrative Pronouns** | This/These<br>That/Those | This/These<br>That/Those | |
| **Indefinite Pronouns** | **Singular:** one, someone, everyone, anyone, another, either, neither, each, anything, everything, nothing, nobody, no one, somebody, something, none (meaning not one) | **Plural:**<br>both, few, several, many, most, others | **Singular or Plural:**<br>all, some, everybody |

The second type of Pronoun is called a *Relative Pronoun*. By definition, a Relative Pronoun refers to a preceding word in the Sentence and connects (relates) that word to the rest of the Sentence (hence, relative). This definition is a bit wordy, but it becomes clearer as you work with it. Normally, these Relative Pronouns are the nasty twins, "who and whom." Other Relative Pronouns are "which and that," but there is no choice of form with "which and that" except in a restrictive and non-restrictive sense.

Remember Pronouns take the place of Nouns. Personal Pronouns are self-explanatory, but how could "who and whom" be Pronouns? How could they take the place of a Noun? The following Sentence will answer that question as well as validate the definition:

Example: The coach praised the boys who ran the relay.

See how "who" takes the place of the word "boys" in the Sentence? If we had no Relative Pronouns, a writer would have to make two Sentences here. "The coach praised the boys." "The boys ran the relay." Hence, "who" takes the place of "boys," and relates "boys" to the rest of the Sentence. That's what a Relative (re-lative) Pronoun does. That's simple, you say. Sure it is.

Here is some more good news! The paradigm for Relative Pronouns is much simpler than the Personal Pronoun Paradigm. See Table 7.

Table 8. Relative Pronoun Paradigm

| Nominative Case For Subjects | Objective Case For Objects | Possessive Case For Ownership |
|---|---|---|
| WHO | WHOM | WHOSE |

Now let's try the simple Three—Step—Drop on Relative Pronouns.

1.  Mom praised the girls *who*/whom cooked the burgers.

    In Relative Pronouns, we are only interested *in what Sentence Part the Pronoun plays within the Clause.* The Clause in which a Relative Pronoun appears is called a Relative Clause. "Who/whom cooked the burgers" is a Relative Clause. Review the definition of a Clause. It is one of the Big Three, along with Sentence and Phrase. (See Chapter 2.)

    We could mark out, and sometimes it helps to do so, "Mom praised the girls," because we care only about what goes on inside the Relative Clause.

Three—Step—Drop:

Step 1: What Sentence Part does the Pronoun play in the Relative Clause? The Pronoun is the Subject of the Clause.

Step 2: Subjects require the Nominative Case.

Step 3: The correct Pronoun form is *who*. One—Two—Three. No guesswork!

2.  The tourist, who/*whom* we transported, arrived safely.

Three—Step—Drop:

Step 1: What Sentence Part does the Pronoun play in the Relative Clause? "We" is the Subject of Relative Clause; "transported" is the Predicate; now, ask "what or whom." And we have an answer—a Direct Object.

Step 2: Direct Objects require the Objective Case.

Step 3: The correct Pronoun form is *whom*. One—Two—Three. No guesswork!

3.  I don't know who/*whom* the president appointed.

Mark out "I don't know."

Step 1: What Sentence Part does the Pronoun play in the Relative Clause? The president appointed whom. The Pronoun is a Direct Object.

Step 2: Direct Objects require the Objective Case.

Step 3: The correct Pronoun form is *whom*.

4.  He is the player *who*/whom, coaches say, will be All-American.

Careful here! You have a parenthetical element—an element not needed for a group of words to be a Sentence. It is "coaches say." Mark it out. Also, you can line out, "He is the player." *All we are interested in is what part the Relative Pronoun plays within the Relative Clause, that is, what is the Sentence Part of the Relative Pronoun.* Now go through your steps.

Step 1: The Pronoun "who" is used as the Subject.

Step 2: Subjects require the Nominative Case.

Step 3: The correct Pronoun form is *who*.

If you had not lined out the parenthetical element, "coaches say," most likely you would have analyzed the Sentence as follows: "Coaches" = Subject; "say" = Predicate; whom = Direct Object. Wrong! Think through this example again. Be ready for Sentence 5.

5.  I sought the mechanic *who*/whom, Barbara claims, is the best.

> We have the same scenario here. "Barbara claims" is parenthetical; hence, it does not enter into the reasoning process.
>
> Step 1: The Pronoun "who" is used as the Subject.
>
> Step 2: Subjects require the Nominative Case.
>
> Step 3: The correct Pronoun form is *who*.
>
> Sometimes a parenthetical element will be several words long. For example, "Who do you think will win?" "Do you think" is parenthetical and the isolated Clause is "who will win."

6.  The woman *whose*/who's purse was stolen, wept. How is the Pronoun used? It is used to show ownership; hence, Possessive Case: correct Pronoun form is "*whose*." One—Two—Three.

7.  Give the clothes to *whoever*/whomever needs them.

> Watch out! Slow down a bit. This requires a good background plus good reasoning. *Remember we are only interested in what takes place within the Relative Clause.* Anything that comes before or after the Relative Clause can be lined out. I call this, "narrowing the fishing hole." Draw a line through "Give the clothes to"— and what do you have? "whoever/whomever needs them."
>
> Step 1: How is the Pronoun used? It is used as the Subject.
>
> Step 2: Subjects require the Nominative Case.
>
> Step 3: The correct Pronoun form is *whoever*. (There is no difference in the rule about the "ever" being attached to the Pronoun.) The isolated Clause is "whoever needs them." Good.

The third type of Pronoun is called an *Interrogative Pronoun.* By definition, it is simply a Pronoun used to ask a question. The Interrogative

Pronoun Paradigm is the same as the Relative Pronoun Paradigm. "Who" is the Nominative Case; "Whom" is the Objective Case; and "Whose" is the Possessive Case.

Table 9. Interrogative Pronoun Paradigm

| Nominative Case For Subjects | Objective Case For Objects | Possessive Case For Ownership |
|---|---|---|
| WHO | WHOM | WHOSE |

Let's nail down the Interrogative Pronouns in question.

1. *Who*/whom mailed the letters?

   Step 1: What Sentence Part is played by the Pronoun? It is used as the Subject.

   Step 2: Subjects require the Nominative Case.

   Step 3: The correct Pronoun form is *who.*

2. With who/*whom* will you sail?

   Step 1: "With" is a Preposition; hence, the Pronoun is the Object of a Preposition.

   Step 2: Objects of Preposition require the Objective Case.

   Step 3: The correct Pronoun form is *whom. When you can answer question number one in the Three—Step—Drop, you are home free!* "What is the Sentence Part played by the Pronoun?" In other words, how is it used in the structure of the Sentence? Subject, Direct Object, Indirect Object, Object of a Preposition, and so forth. I bet you've figured that out by now.

3. Who/*Whom* shall we send?

   Step 1: What is the Sentence Part played by the Pronoun? Let's analyze. "We" is the Subject, "shall send" is the Predicate. We shall send what or whom? Do we have an answer? Sure. It is the Direct Object. In this case, the Direct Object is the word "whom."

   Step 2: Direct Objects require the Objective Case.

Step 3: The correct Pronoun form is *whom*. One—Two—Three.

4. Did the coach say to work with *whoever*/whomever arrives? Careful. You have a Relative Clause embedded in this Interrogative Sentence. And when this happens, follow the rule of the Relative Clause, that is to say, "How is the Pronoun used within the Relative Clause?" We are concerned only with what goes on within the Relative Clause. Draw a line from the beginning of the Sentence through the word "with"; if you do not, you will think that the Preposition governs the case of the Pronoun, making it the Object of the Preposition and the following case Objective and the correct Pronoun form "whomever." Wrong!

Now, we will fish in a smaller fishing hole; "Whoever/whomever arrives."

Step 1: The Pronoun is used as the Subject (the topic of the Clause).

Step 2: Subjects require the Nominative Case.

Step 3: The correct Pronoun form is *whoever*. A similar Sentence was read incorrectly in a recent national newscast, meaning that neither the news anchor nor anyone in his editorial staff knew about the Three—Step—Drop. The blue suit and power tie could not hide the glaring error. You will not make this mistake!

5. Should I ask *whoever*/whomever is in charge for a ticket? Once again, you have a Relative Clause embedded in this Interrogative Sentence. So beware! Mark a line through "Should I ask." This will keep you from thinking that the Pronoun is used as a Direct Object. The false reasoning would go like this; "I" is the Subject, "should ask" is the Predicate, and "what or whom" is the Direct Object; hence, Objective Case, correct Pronoun form should be "whomever." Wrong! In the smaller fishing hole, we have "whoever/whomever is in charge for a ticket."

Step 1: "Whoever" is the Subject of the Clause.

Step 2: Subjects require the Nominative Case.

Step 3: The correct Pronoun form is *whoever*.

The fourth type of Pronoun is called a *Reflexive Pronoun.* By definition, it is a two-part (compound) Pronoun used only in the Objective Case and means the same thing as the Subject of the Sentence. Take myself, for example; My+self = myself. See how it is a two-part Pronoun? Take a look at the Reflexive Pronoun Paradigm, Table 10.

Table 10. Reflexive Pronoun Paradigm

| Nominative Case Subject; Predicate Pronoun | Objective Case Direct Object; Indirect Object; Object of a Preposition | Possessive Case Ownership; Used Before Gerund |
|---|---|---|
| | Myself                 Ourselves<br>Yourself                Yourselves<br>Himself/Herself/Itself    Themselves | |

Of course, the first thing you notice about this paradigm is that the Pronoun cannot be used except in the Objective Case. It cannot be used as the Subject. You cannot say, "Myself went to town." Neither can you use it in the Possessive Case. You cannot say, "The coat is myselfs." But the Reflexive Pronoun is tricky and devious. Hear the Sheriff on TV responding to the question: "How did you catch the criminals?" "Well, Deputy Jones and myself went to the residence of the suspects." "Myself" sounds so humble and so correct. The fact remains that you cannot make a Subject out of a Reflexive Pronoun; you cannot say, "Myself went to the residence." The Reflexive Pronoun has no Nominative Case. See Table 10. People seem to cower from the good, wholesome Personal Pronoun "I." This is another example of why you cannot trust *sound* as your guide in matters of Proper Form.

Another trap with the Reflexive (Latin for "waves back") Pronoun is that it must mean *exactly* what the Subject means, or else you cannot use a Reflexive Pronoun. Let's deal with these Reflexive Pronouns to make sure they can never trick us again!

Examples:

- The call was for Professor Jones or *me*/myself.

Is "myself" the same as the Subject "call"? Certainly not; then you must use the old-fashioned Personal Pronoun "me." The call was for Professor Jones or *me.*

Even more devious is the use of a Reflexive Pronoun with an Imperative Mood Verb (which I will cover in the next chapter). But while we are close, let's glance at it.

- Contact Professor Jones or myself/*me* if you have questions.

    The understood Subject of every Imperative Mood Verb (command) is "You." Hence, is "myself" the same as the Subject "you"? Certainly not. Therefore, you must use the old-fashioned, ego-centered Pronoun, "me." (You) contact Professor Jones or *me* if you have questions.

One last warning about Reflexive Pronouns—there is no such word as "hisself," and there is no such word as "theirselves." Review Reflexive Pronoun paradigm, Table 10. These non words are not included.

Here are some examples of correct usage of the Reflexive Pronoun:

- *I* prefer to visit the islands *myself.* (Reflexive Pronoun "myself" is the same as the Subject, "I.")
- *You* could not have done better *yourself.* (Reflexive Pronoun "yourself" is the same as Subject, "you.")
- The *men* lifted *themselves* out of the cave with a rope. (Reflexive Pronoun "themselves" is the same as the Subject, "men.")
- *We* do not ask recognition for *ourselves.* (Reflexive Pronoun "ourselves" is the same as the Subject, "we.")
- The *woman* preferred to pay the debt *herself.* (Reflexive Pronoun "herself" is the same as the Subject, "woman.")

In each of the previous Sentences, draw a line from the Reflexive Pronoun to the Noun or Pronoun to which it "waves back." Good! You've conquered Mr. Reflexive Pronoun. The next Pronoun is even easier.

Pronoun number five is a brother to the Reflexive Pronoun. It is called an *Intensive Pronoun.* The same paradigm holds true for the Intensive Pronoun. By definition, an Intensive Pronoun is a compound (two-part) Personal Pronoun used only in the Objective Case that *emphasizes its antecedent* (the word that comes before it).

Table 11. Intensive Pronoun Paradigm

| Nominative Case Subject; Predicate Pronoun | Objective Case Direct Object; Indirect Object; Object of a Preposition | Possessive Case Ownership; Used before Gerund |
|---|---|---|
| | Myself                Ourselves<br>Yourself              Yourselves<br>Himself/Herself/Itself  Themselves | |

Here are some examples of the "Intensive" Pronoun. Notice how the *Intensive Pronoun* emphasizes its antecedent.

1. I, *myself*, prefer hot dogs.
2. He, *himself*, (not hisself) is the culprit.
3. You, *yourself*, must bear the burden.
4. The soldiers, *themselves*, (not theirselves) should be saluted.
5. "It is He who has made us and not we *ourselves*."

Now, draw a line from the Intensive Pronoun to its antecedent.

Pronoun number six is called a Demonstrative Pronoun. It comes from the Latin word, "Demonstrare" which means "to point out."
If you were lying on a yacht you might say, "This is high-class living." "This" is a Pronoun. If you said, "This vacation is high-class living," "This" would be an Adjective telling which vacation. When the Noun is missing entirely, the substitute word is a Pronoun. In this case, it is called a *Demonstrative Pronoun* because it points out or designates something.

If you were looking at a diamond ring, you might say, "*This* is beautiful." "This" would be a Demonstrative Pronoun, referring to a single item close at hand. If you had several rings, you might say, "These are beautiful," referring to a plurality of items close at hand. "This" and "These" are Demonstrative Pronouns. But that's not all.

"That" is a singular Demonstrative Pronoun for things far removed. If you saw a Lexus from your window, you might say, "*That* is classy." If you saw more than one Lexus, you might say, "*Those* are classy." Once again, this is a Demonstrative (point out) Pronoun. My little Latin professor who was four feet eight inches tall, used to say, "Grandma was right on when she said, 'This (here) and That (there).'"

*This* and *These* are Demonstrative Pronouns for things close at hand. *That* and *Those* are Demonstrative Pronouns for things far removed.

Lest you be lulled to sleep with the simplicity of these last few Pronouns, here comes a dandy. It is called an Indefinite Pronoun. Its definition fits its name, as do most of these Pronouns, because it refers to "*persons or things in general, as opposed to specific persons or things.*"

Some of these Indefinite Pronouns are singular: Each, One, Someone, No one, Nobody, Nothing, Something, Anybody, None (meaning not one) and so forth.

Some of these Indefinite Pronouns are plural: Many, Few, Several, Both, Most, Others, and so forth.

You can see the singularity and plurality easily. There are a few Indefinite Pronouns which can be singular or plural according to the context of the Sentence: All, Some, and Everybody are the most prominent. For example, "All (singular) I want is a hamburger." But, "All (plural) are wanting a hamburger."

"Everybody (singular) read his/her favorite poem."

"Everybody (plural) came to the meeting, but everybody did not stay."

"Some (singular) assembly is required."

"Some (plural) contributed; some did not contribute."

The kicker with Indefinite Pronouns is that the Predicate (Verb) which follows them must "Agree" with the Pronoun in number. If the Indefinite Pronoun is singular, then the Predicate (Verb) must be singular; likewise with plurals. I saw a sign in an antique shop that read, "Six months ago I couldn't spell Professor, and now I are one." What made that funny was that the Subject "I" was singular and the Predicate (Verb) "are" was plural. I will discuss Verbs in detail later but you can get the idea of Subject/Verb Agreement from the antique shop illustration.

Another challenge presented by the Indefinite Pronoun is that the singularity or plurality of this Pronoun determines the singularity or plurality of all other Pronouns that follow. (See Sentences number eight and number nine below.)

Here are some examples:    (Remember, they demand Subject/ Verb Agreement and also dictate the singularity or plurality of all other Pronouns that follow in the Sentence.)

1. *Each* (singular) carry/*carries* a rifle. (Carries; he/she/it carries, singular Verb)

2. *Few* (plural) *carry*/carries a rifle. (Carry; they carry, plural Verb)

3. *One* (singular) of the roses *is*/are pink. "One" is the Subject; "is" is singular; hence, "is" is correct. (It is.)

4. *None* (singular; meaning not one) of the players *was*/were accepted. "None" is the Subject; "none" is singular; hence "was" is correct. (He/she was not accepted.)

5. *Each* (singular) of the flowers smell/*smells* sweet. "Each" is the Subject; it is singular; hence, "smells" is correct. (It smells.)

6. *Few* (plural) *forsake*/forsakes their homeland. (They forsake.)

7. *Someone* left *his*/*her* their coat. ("Someone" is singular; hence, *his/ her* is correct.)

8. *Each* should plan for *his*/*her* their retirement. ("Each" is singular; hence, *his/her* is correct.)

9. *One* never *learns*/learn as much as *he*/*she*/they can. ("One" is singular; hence, "learns" and "he/she" are correct.)

Now for the hands-on work. There are several worksheets attached. They will not take long, but I suggest you go through them cautiously— *never resorting to sound as a guide for Proper Form.* Pronouns are toughies because they have a multiplicity of forms.

Instead of guessing, use the simple Three—Step—Drop and retain your poise. Review the notes and Pronoun Paradigm, Table 7, if necessary. Once again, here is the Three—Step—Drop:

1. What is the Sentence Part played by the Pronoun? (Subject, Direct Object, Indirect Object, Object of a Preposition)

2. What Pronoun Case is correct for this Sentence Part? (Nominative, Objective, Possessive)

3. What is the correct Pronoun form?

Table 12. Pronoun Worksheet

## PERSONAL PRONOUNS:

1. Mom called she/her and he/him to lunch.

2. The party was a surprise for they/them.

3. If you need help, call Dad or myself/me.

4. That is Jane's mother, standing next to she/her and her husband.

5. I walked with Jake and she/her.

6. He insisted on paying the bill hisself/himself.

7. The puppy rode with Dad and I/me.

8. The professor asked she/her and he/him to recite.

9. Mom and I sat next to he/him and his wife.

10. Between you and I/me, Kevin and I/myself were chosen for the committee.

## RELATIVE PRONOUNS:

1. Flags flew for the soldiers who/whom were victorious in battle.

2. The players, who/whom we had contacted, did well.

3. I found the farmer who/whom people say raises the best corn.

4. The trainer shot the lion that/that had escaped.

5. The boy, who/whom your mother prefers, is named Jack Johnson.

6. The coach will be pleased with whoever/whomever finishes first.

7. The man, who's/whose arm was bleeding, tried to rescue others.

8. Give the award to whoever/whomever deserves it.

9. Susan did not know who/whom the board appointed.

10. Dr. Benson is the surgeon who/whom we recommended.

## INTERROGATIVE PRONOUNS:

1. Who's/Whose coat is this?

2. Who/Whom addressed the envelope?

3. For who/whom did you request money?

4. Did the instructor say to work with whoever/whomever arrives?

5. Should I ask whoever/whomever is in charge for a ticket?

6. Who/Whom paid the bill?

7. Who/Whom shall we send?

8. With who/whom will you sail?

9. Who/Whom do you think will win?

## INDEFINITE PRONOUNS:

1. Not one student turned in his/her their paper.

2. Each leaves/leave a legacy.

3. Many leaves/leave houses and land.

4. One of the girls has/have gone.

5. Few forsake his/her their homelands.

6. None (not one) of the players was/were accepted.

7. Nothing hurt/hurts like a boil.

8. Each supports his/her their candidate.

9. All (the one thing) I want is/are a watermelon.

10. Both secretaries presented his/her their paperwork.

## REFLEXIVE PRONOUNS:

1. John wanted to fix the car hisself/himself.

2. The ladies did not ask recognition for themselves/theirselves.

3. My sister wanted to bake the cake herself/herself.

4. We do not glorify ourself/ourselves.

5. He was by himself/hisself when the wreck happened.

## INTENSIVE PRONOUNS:

1. I, myself/me, prefer administration.

2. The councilmen, themselves/theirselves, should be honored.

3. You (singular), yourself/yourselves, must bear the burden.

4. He, hisself/himself, was the culprit.

Table 13. Answers for Pronoun Worksheet
Italicized words are correct.

## PERSONAL PRONOUNS:

1. Mom called she/*her* and he/*him* to lunch. ✓

2. The party was a surprise for they/*them*. ✓

3. If you need help, call Dad or myself/*me*. ✓

4. That is Jane's mother, standing next to she/*her* and her husband. ✓

5. I walked with Jake and she/*her*. ✓

6. He insisted on paying the bill hisself/*himself*. ✓

7. The puppy rode with Dad and I/*me*. ✓

8. The professor asked she/*her* and he/*him* to recite. ✓

9. Mom and I sat next to he/*him* and his wife. ✓

10. Between you and I/*me*, Kevin and *I*/myself were chosen for the committee. ✓

## RELATIVE PRONOUNS:

1. Flags flew for the soldiers *who*/whom were victorious in battle. ✓

2. The players, who/*whom* we had contacted, did well. ✓

3. I found the farmer *who*/whom people say raises the best corn. ✓

4. The trainer shot the lion *that*/*that* had escaped. ✓

5. The boy, who/*whom* your mother prefers, is named Jack Johnson. ✓

6. The coach will be pleased with *whoever*/whomever finishes first.

7. The man, who's/*whose* arm was bleeding, tried to rescue others. ✓

8. Give the award to *whoever*/whomever deserves it. ✓

9. Susan did not know who/*whom* the board appointed. ✓

10. Dr. Benson is the surgeon who/*whom* we recommended. ✓

## INTERROGATIVE PRONOUNS:

1. Who's/*Whose* coat is this? ✓

2. *Who*/Whom addressed the envelope? ✓

3. For who/*whom* did you request money? ✓

4. Did the instructor say to work with *whoever*/whomever arrives? ✓

5. Should I ask *whoever*/whomever is in charge for a ticket? ✓

6. *Who*/Whom paid the bill? ✓

7. Who/*Whom* shall we send? ✓

8. With who/*whom* will you sail? ✓

9. *Who*/Whom do you think will win? ✓

### INDEFINITE PRONOUNS:

1. Not one student turned in *his/her* their paper. ✓

2. Each *leaves*/leave a legacy. ✓

3. Many leaves/*leave* houses and land. ✓

4. One of the girls *has*/have gone. ✓

5. Few forsake his/her *their* homelands. ✓

6. None (not one) of the players *was*/were accepted. ✓

7. Nothing hurt/*hurts* like a boil. ✓

8. Each supports *his/her* their candidate. ✓

9. All (the one thing) I want *is*/are a watermelon. ✓

10. Both secretaries presented his/her *their* paperwork. ✓

### REFLEXIVE PRONOUNS:

1. John wanted to fix the car hisself/*himself*. ✓

2. The ladies did not ask recognition for *themselves*/theirselves. ✓

3. My sister wanted to bake the cake herself/*herself*. ✓

4. We do not glorify ourself/*ourselves*. ✓

5. He was by *himself*/hisself when the wreck happened. ✓

### INTENSIVE PRONOUNS:

1. I, *myself*/me, prefer administration. ✓

2. The councilmen, *themselves*/theirselves, should be honored. ✓

3. You (singular), *yourself*/yourselves, must bear the burden. ✓

4. He, him/*himself*, was the culprit. ✓

LET'S VISIT!

You've reached an important milestone in your quest for Proper Form. You have learned the difference between the eight Parts of Speech (Noun, Pronoun, Verb, Adjective, Adverb, Preposition, Conjunction, and Interjection) and the Parts of a Sentence (Subject, Predicate, Direct Object, Indirect Object, and Object of a Preposition). You have pushed some grammatical debris aside and have begun to emerge from your career-threatening suffocation.

You've learned about Pronouns and adopted a fail-proof way of determining which form of the Pronoun is correct. I call it the Three—Step—Drop, but you may call it anything you wish as long as you follow the three steps:

1. What is the Sentence Part played by the Pronoun?

2. What Pronoun Case is correct for this Sentence Part?

3. What is the correct Pronoun form?

*As you have learned, Step number one is by far the most important.* The others follow easily.

By now you should feel confident in your pursuit of Proper Form. You have made good progress. Remember to take slow, sure, steps and nail everything down before proceeding. You do not need to go into the next study (Verbs) without a break. How about a chocolate almond milkshake and a cheeseburger? They go great with Proper Form!

# Chapter 4

## Focusing on Verbs

A *Verb* is a word that shows action (or state of being). Verbs have *Mood, Voice, Person, Number,* and *Tense* which will be treated in simple detail on the following pages. Do not panic! Treat these exactly as you did the Nouns and Pronouns—one-step-at-a-time.

MOOD OF A VERB: reveals the writer's or speaker's attitude toward what he/she is saying, (in other words, his mood).

There are three Verb Moods:

1. Indicative Mood:

   This Mood simply makes a statement. For example, "The car is beautiful." "Let's go to the game." "Johns Hopkins is a world-class hospital." Probably 90 percent of the Verbs you use will be in the Indicative Mood. Self-definition is applicable here; it simply *indicates* something or makes a statement.

2. Imperative Mood:     IMPERATOR = COMMANDER

   This Mood gives a command (from the Latin word, *Imperator,* meaning "commander"). When an officer enters the meeting area where five hundred soldiers are standing, he simply says, "Sit." Sit is an Imperative Mood of the Verb. When a professor tells his class, "*Lay* your papers on the desk," he is using the Imperative Mood of the Verb. The understood Subject of every

Imperative Mood Verb is "you." (You) stand; (You) sit; (You) lay your papers on the desk.

3. Subjunctive Mood:

This Mood is used when a statement is contrary to fact (untrue), or when something is wished, desired, or possible. Normally, it involves the changing of "was" to "were," ("was" being the Indicative Mood and "were" being the Subjunctive Mood). The best example of the Subjunctive Mood to be used when the action is contrary to fact is this: "If I *were* you, I would buy the red car." Obviously, I am not you. This is contrary to fact (untrue). Hence, we cannot use the Indicative Mood and say, "If I was you." Also, the Subjunctive Mood is used when something is wished: "I wish Jack *were* my doctor." He is not; hence, contrary to fact. "I wish Clyde *were* my friend." He is not; hence, contrary to fact. My third grade Reader had a picture of three children sitting on a wharf looking out to sea. The title of the book was *If I Were Going*. Obviously the children were not going; hence, contrary to fact. Here's a kicker. What if you do not know whether the Sentence is contrary to fact or not? *If you do not know, use the Indicative Mood.* Example: if someone brought you a precious stone and asked how much you thought it would be worth— and you had no way of knowing what type of stone it was—you would tell him/her, "If this *was* a diamond, it would be worth $1,000." But, if you knew that the stone was a Cubic Zirconia, you would reply, "If this *were* a diamond (contrary to fact), it would be worth $1000." Since "were" is used in the Past Tense, it is called a Past Subjunctive. There is a Present Subjunctive "be" which presents no major problem in Proper Form. Here is an example of the Present Subjunctive, "The committee suggested that the chief operating officer *be* retained."

The Subjunctive Mood has been on its deathbed for many years. Even some English majors are unfamiliar with it, but misuse of it sends out the message, "Untutored, Untutored,"—so let's deal with it and use it correctly.

VOICE OF A VERB: There are two Verb Voices.

1. Active Voice: Where the Subject does the acting

2. Passive Voice: Where the Subject receives the action

(The terms almost identify themselves.)

I carry = Active Voice. The Subject (I) does the acting.

I am carried = Passive Voice. The Subject (I) receives the action.

You have seen = Active Voice. The Subject (you) does the acting.

You have been seen = Passive Voice. The Subject (you) receives the action.

PERSON OF A VERB: the Person of the Verb shows who or what does the action. This is a bit misleading, because these are actually Pronouns, and not part of the Verb (action word) itself. You will recognize these *Persons of the Verb* as being your friends from the Nominative Case of the Personal Pronoun. They are as follows:

| Singular | Plural |
|---|---|
| First Person = I (Person speaking.) | We = (Persons speaking.) |
| Second Person = You (Person spoken to.) | You = (Persons spoken to.) |
| Third Person = He/She/it (Person spoken about.) | They = (Persons spoken about.) |

Before you will have finished this study of Verbs, these Pronouns, serving as Persons of the Verb, will roll "trippingly off your tongue" as Shakespeare said.

NUMBER OF A VERB: The number of the Verb is either Singular or Plural.

| Singular | Plural |
|---|---|
| I | We |
| You | You |
| He/She/it | They |

The Number of a Verb is no problem. Here comes the problem—the Tense of a Verb and the Conjugational Scheme. So, keep your plow in the ground.

TENSE OF A VERB: deals with the *time* of the action of the Verb.

In English, we have six Tenses (time designations) of a Verb—as do Latin and Greek. English Tenses are as follows:

1. Present Tense: "I *sing* in the shower."

2. Past Tense: "I *sang* in the shower."

3. Future Tense: "I *shall sing* in the shower."

"Shall" is often used as a Helping Verb in the 1st Person Singular. "I shall sing," and the 1st Person Plural, "We shall sing." While both "will" and "shall" denote future action, "will" is often associated with strong feeling.

It is not enough to slice time into three pieces (Present, Past, Future); we need to slice time into three more, even thinner slices to show an action *that has just happened (Present Perfect Tense), an action that happened at a definite time in the past (Past Perfect Tense), or an action that will happen at a definite time in the future (Future Perfect Tense).* These slices of time are made possible by the so-called "Perfect Tenses"; the Present Perfect Tense, the Past Perfect Tense, and the Future Perfect Tense of the Verb.

4. Present Perfect Tense: This Tense deals with an action that has just been completed or is continuing. It uses the helping Verb "have/has."

The football announcer will say, "The quarterback *has* (Present Perfect Tense) thrown another touchdown pass," (an action that has just been completed). The announcer could be grammatically correct by saying, "The quarterback *threw* (Past Tense) another touchdown pass." But this does not slice time thinly enough, which is the reason that the *Perfect Tenses* (Present Perfect, Past Perfect, Future Perfect) exist. The newsman will say, "The water has gone over the dam," (an action which has just been completed). The newsman could be grammatically correct by saying, "The water went (Past Tense) over the dam." But, it would not slice time thinly enough.

The Present Perfect Tense is also used when an action is continuing. "The Joneses *have traveled* in Alaska for years." See how it shows continuing action? The Past Tense would have said, "The Joneses *traveled* in Europe for years." It would have been grammatically correct, but again it would not have sliced time thinly enough. Here's one last example: "I have sung in the shower for many years," (an action that is continuing). If the Sentence had said, "I sang in the shower for many years," the reader would not know if the singer was continuing to sing or if he had quit singing in the shower.

5. Past Perfect Tense: This Tense deals with an action that has been completed at some "definite" time in the past. It uses the helping Verb "had."

"Jim *had* left town before he heard the news."

"I *had earned* a degree before you were born."

"If the police *had* not come, bloodshed would have occurred."

The football announcer often fails to use this Tense correctly. He says, "If the defensive back *did* not make that tackle, the runner would have scored." The tackle was an action that took place at a definite time in the past, so he should have said, "If the defensive back *had* not made that tackle, the runner would have scored."

6. Future Perfect Tense: This Tense deals with an action that will take place at some "definite" time in the future. It uses the helping Verb "shall/will have."

"You *will have earned* a degree by next summer."

"In three months, spring *will have come* and the flowers *will have bloomed.*"

"Before you *will have finished* this book, you will know how to conjugate Verbs."

In review, there are six Tenses of a Verb. These Tenses exist to show the time of the action of a Verb. The Present Tense, the Past Tense, and the Future Tense are self-explanatory as they indicate the time of the action of the Verb. The Present Perfect, Past Perfect, and Future Perfect Tenses (the so-called Perfect Tenses) slice the time of the action of a Verb into three even smaller segments. These Perfect Tenses are relatively simple. The Present Perfect Tense shows an action that has just been completed or is continuing. Its helping Verb is "have/has." The Past Perfect Tense shows an action that had been completed at some definite time in the past. Its helping Verb is "had." The Future Perfect Tense shows an action that will have been completed at some definite time in the future. Its helping Verb is "shall/will have."

Now, let's examine the big old term that has been lurking in the shadows—"*Conjugational Scheme.*" In the words of the old Proverb, "Its bark is much worse than its bite." Let's open the gate and go in together. Let's see just how big and bad this dog is. All right?

To teach you how to express time, we do what is called CONJUGATING A VERB. The Latin word for wife is "*conjunx*," meaning "to join." The suffix "—ate" means the "process of." Therefore, when we *Conjugate a Verb* we are in the process of joining (or marrying) the Pronoun to the Verb itself. Easy here, this is not tough. An example will clear it up immediately. Let's conjugate (marry the Pronoun to the Verb) a Verb in the Present Tense. Try the Verb "see."

Table 14. Conjugation of the Verb "see" in the Present Tense

|  | **Singular** | **Plural** |
|---|---|---|
| 1st Person of Verb | I (Verb) = see | We = see |
| 2nd Person of Verb | You (Verb) = see | You = see |
| 3rd Person of Verb | He/she/it (Verb) = sees | They = see |

Notice how you have joined the Person of the Verb (I, you, he/she/it, and we/you/they) with the Verb "see" to express time. The time you expressed was the present. You will notice also that the 3rd Person Singular uses an "s" on the Verb, hence, "*sees.*" (He/she/it sees.) Now, conjugate the Verb "ride" in the Present Tense.

I _____ ride

you _____ ride

HE/SHE/IT _____ rides

You joined the Person of the Verb with the Verb "ride" to express the *time* of the action of the Verb! The time you expressed was the Present. Good! I knew you could do it. Understanding how to express time is vital for the knowledgeable person as he/she participates in a learned society that expects and appreciates clear, pinpointed expression.

Remember, the main reason for conjugating a Verb is that it allows us to pinpoint the time of the Verb's action. In addition, by learning to conjugate a Verb, you learn Subject/Verb Agreement, Active/Passive

Voice, as well as proper use of auxiliary Verbs (helping Verbs). So, Verb conjugation is a great investment of your time. You might say, "I did well on the Present Tense Conjugation, how many Tenses remain?" There are six Tenses in the Active Voice and six Tenses in the Passive Voice—a total of twelve. Here's the good news! We have some building blocks that will simplify the conjugation of any Verb. The building blocks are called the *Three Principal Parts of a Verb*. For example, the Three Principal Parts (Stems) of the Verb "see" are see—saw—seen.

Table 15. The Three Principal Parts of a Verb

| Present Stem | Past Stem | Past Participle Stem |
|---|---|---|
| See | Saw | Seen |

We will use these building blocks (Stems) to form all six Tenses of the Active Voice and all six Tenses of the Passive Voice. We will proceed one—sure—step—at—a—time. It will be like putting a simple puzzle together.

The only way to learn to conjugate a Verb is to memorize the THREE PRINCIPAL PARTS OF A VERB. If you don't know the Three Principal Parts, a good dictionary will give them. Once you have memorized them, you can use these building blocks to conjugate any Verb in the English language. My grandmother chanted the Three Principal Parts of a Verb garnered from the textbooks that her children had brought home. She was self-educated but was learning the building blocks of the conjugational scheme so that the she could pinpoint the "time" of the action of a Verb. Again, if we know the Three Principal Parts of a Verb, we can conjugate any Verb through all its Tenses. If I ask Bubba how we are going to utilize Three Principal Parts in twelve Tenses, his answer is always quick and positive, "It's four." This little ridiculous rampage is designed to reassure you that you do not lose your sense of humor when you choose to use Proper Form. You will not forsake smiling, lose your personality, or begin to walk like Mrs. McGuillacuddy. A young lady once commented in class, "My friends don't talk in Proper Form; and if I talk like this, they'll look at me askance." I replied, "This may happen, but rest assured in future days, the askance glance will have to be upward."

It seems that you need a breather! Come up for a bit of air, and then we will dive deeply into Verb Conjugation. Enchiladas, tortilla chips, salsa, and cheese dip should give you the boost you need!

There's a toy store called "Build a Bear" where children put their own Teddy Bears together. In so doing, they have a total understanding of how the bear is made. Once you build the conjugational structure of a Verb, you'll know exactly what goes in where and how it is stitched together. The *Conjugational Scheme* to the student of Proper Form is equivalent to the multiplication table for the mathematician. Both are indispensible to the student as he/she climbs higher into the discipline.  For this reason, Verb Conjugation will be presented clinically and repetitiously.

In the toy store, the first thing children are shown is what a "finished bear" looks like. This bear has all of its limbs, furry parts, and all of its stitches and buttons. With that in mind, get out your "finished bear"—the Verb conjugation of "see-saw-seen" listed in the following Table, Table 16. Is it before you? All right! Let's begin to build. I will show you exactly how to form each Tense. Hang in there. You can do this!

*[handwritten: 3rd person singular verb]*

Table 16. Verb Conjugation Paradigm of the Verb "see"

Three Principal Parts : SEE—SAW—SEEN

Active Voice *[handwritten: – SUBJECT DOES ACTING (3RD)]*

*[handwritten left margin: PRESENT STEM]*

| Present Tense ① | | Present Perfect Tense *[JUST COMPLETED]* | |
|---|---|---|---|
| I see | We see | I have seen | We have seen |
| You see | You see | You have seen | You have seen |
| He/She/It sees | They see | He/She/It has seen | They have seen |

*[handwritten: USE "HAS" or "HAVE"]*
*[handwritten right margin: PAST PARTIC. STEM +]*

*[handwritten left margin: PAST STEM]*

| Past Tense ② | | Past Perfect Tense *[USE "HAD" at one definite time in past]* | |
|---|---|---|---|
| I saw | We saw | I had seen | We had seen |
| You saw | You saw | You had seen | You had seen |
| He/She/It saw | They saw | He/She/It had seen | They had seen |

*[handwritten right margin: (3RD) PAST PARTIC. +]*

*[handwritten left margin: PRESENT STEM + "WILL or SHALL"]*

| Future Tense ③ | | Future Perfect Tense *[USE "WILL/SHALL HAVE"]* | |
|---|---|---|---|
| I shall/will see | We shall/will see | I shall/will have seen | We shall/will have seen |
| You will see | You will see | You will have seen | You will have seen |
| He/She/It will see | They will see | He/She/It will have seen | They will have seen |

*[handwritten: WILL TAKE PLACE AT A CERTAIN TIME]*
*[handwritten right margin: (3) PAST PARTIC. +]*

*[handwritten: ALL USE PAST PARTICIPLE STEM]*

## Passive Voice *(handwritten: SUBJECT RECEIVES ACTION)*

| Present Tense (7) | | Present Perfect Tense (10) | |
|---|---|---|---|
| I am seen | We are seen | I have been seen | We have been seen |
| You are seen | You are seen | You have been seen | You have been seen |
| He/She/It is seen | They are seen | He/She/It has been seen | They have been seen |

*[handwritten: + has/have & been]*

| Past Tense (8) | | Past Perfect Tense (11) | |
|---|---|---|---|
| I was seen | We were seen | I had been seen | We had been seen |
| You were seen | You were seen | You had been seen | You had been seen |
| He/She/It was seen | They were seen | He/She/It had been seen | They had been seen |

*[handwritten: + had & been]*

| Future Tense (9) | | Future Perfect Tense (12) | |
|---|---|---|---|
| I shall/will be seen | We shall/will be seen | I shall/will have been seen | We shall/will have been seen |
| You will be seen | You will be seen | You will have been seen | You will have been seen |
| He/She/It will be seen | They will be seen | He/She/It will have been seen | They will have been seen |

*[handwritten: + shall/will have been]*

Now, let's take the Tenses one by one and see how each is formed.

(1) Look at the Present Tense: Active Voice, Table 16.

"I see," and so forth.

- It is built upon "The Present Stem" (1st Principal Part) = "See."

- Note: the 3rd Person Singular is - he/she/it "*sees.*" It is not "He see"! Consider the following incorrect Sentences: "He carry the groceries." "She see a storm cloud." "It leave a bad taste in your mouth."

- On Table 16, write "Present Stem" in the margin beside Present Tense.

- Time of action of Verb—self-explanatory. It shows action in the present time.

(2) Look at the Past Tense: Active Voice, Table 16.

"I saw," and so forth.

- It is built upon the "Past Stem" (2nd Principal Part) = "Saw."

- On Table 16, write Past Stem in the margin beside Past Tense.

- Time of action of Verb—self-explanatory. It shows action in a past time.

③ Look at the Future Tense: Active Voice, Table 16.

"I shall/will see," and so forth.

- It is built upon the "Present Stem" (1st Principal Part) + "shall/will" = "shall/will See."

- On Table 16, write Present Stem + "shall/will" in the margin beside Future Tense.

- Time of action of Verb—self-explanatory. It shows action in a future time.

④ Look at the Present Perfect Tense: Active Voice, Table 16.

"I have seen," and so forth.

- It is built upon the "Past Participle Stem" (3rd Principal Part) + "have/has." Do not worry about what Past Participle means. When we study Participles, you can learn it easily.

- It requires a Helping Verb—have/has. Note: the 3rd Person Singular is—"He/She/It *has* seen." It is not, "He have seen"! Consider the following incorrect statements: "He have carried." "She have given." "It have rained."

- On Table 16, write 3rd Principal Part + "have/has" in the margin beside Present Perfect Tense.

- Time of action of Verb— it shows an action that has just happened or is continuing.

⑤ Look at the Past Perfect Tense: Active Voice, Table 16.

"I had seen," and so forth.

- It is built upon the "Past Participle Stem" (3rd Principal Part) + had = "had seen."

- It requires a Helping Verb—had.

- On Table 16, write 3rd Principal Part + "had" in the margin beside Past Perfect Tense.

- Time of action of Verb—it shows an action that had taken place at some definite time in the past.

Look at the Future Perfect Tense: Active Voice, Table 16.

"I shall/will have seen," and so forth.

- It is built upon "Past Participle Stem" (3rd Principal Part) + shall/will have = "shall/will have seen."

- It requires a Helping Verb—shall/will have.

- On Table 16, write 3rd Principal Part + "shall/will have" in the margin beside Future Perfect Tense.

- Time of action of Verb—it shows an action that will have taken place at some definite time in the future.

This is a time for sure-footed advancement. I do not want any terms to float over your head and be drawn up into another cloud of debris that will collapse upon you in the future. So, let's go back and review the conjugation of the Active Voice Verb before proceeding. All right? Yes, you do need the review. "But my mind is like a steel trap." True, but as in every human being, it is also like a sieve.

Congratulations! You have learned and reviewed the six Tenses of the Active Voice of a Verb. It is Active because the Subject is doing the action. "I see" = the Subject does the seeing.

Now, let's go to the six Tenses of the Passive Voice. Good news! All six Tenses of the Passive Voice are formed with the Past Participle Stem (3rd Principal Part of a Verb). Since these Verbs are *Passive Voice*, this means that the Subject receives the action—"I am seen," "I was seen," "I will be seen," and so forth.

Look at the Present Tense: Passive Voice, Table 16.

"I am seen," and so forth.

- It is built upon the "Past Participle Stem" (3rd Principal Part) of see—saw—seen.

- Note: I am seen, you are seen, he/she/it "is" seen. Again, beware the 3rd Person Singular.

- On Table 16, write 3rd Principal Part in the margin beside Present Tense.

- Time of action of the Verb—self-explanatory. It shows action in the present time.

Look at <u>Past Tense: Passive Voice</u>, Table 16.

"I was seen," and so forth.

- It is built upon the "Past Participle Stem" (3$^{rd}$ Principal Part) of see—saw—seen.

- On Table 16, write 3$^{rd}$ Principal Part in the margin beside Past Tense.

- Time of action of the Verb—self-explanatory. It shows action in a past time.

 Look at <u>Future Tense: Passive Voice</u>, Table 16.

"I shall/will be seen," and so forth.

- It is built upon the "Past Participle Stem" (3$^{rd}$ Principal Part) of see—saw—seen.

- Note how <u>the word "be" changes the Verb to Passive Voice</u>. "I shall/will see" = Active Voice (the Subject is doing the seeing). But, "I shall/will be seen" = Passive Voice (the Subject is receiving the action).

- On Table 16, write 3$^{rd}$ Principal Part in the margin beside Future Tense.

- Time of action of the Verb—self-explanatory. It shows action in a future time.

10 Look at <u>Present Perfect Tense: Passive Voice</u>, Table 16.

"I have been seen," and so forth.

- It is built upon the "Past Participle Stem" (3$^{rd}$ Principal Part) + <u>have/has + been.</u>

- Note the helping Verb "have/has." The word "been" makes the action go back to the Subject. That's why it is Passive Voice; the Subject receives the action.

- On Table 16, write 3$^{rd}$ Principal Part + have/has + been in the margin beside Present Perfect Tense.

- Time of action of the Verb—it shows an action that has just happened or is continuing.

⑪ Look at Past Perfect Tense: Passive Voice, Table 16.

"I had been seen," and so forth.

- It is built upon the "Past Participle Stem" (3ʳᵈ Principal Part) + had + been.
- Note helping Verb "had." The word "been" makes the action go back to the Subject. That's why it is Passive Voice; the Subject receives the action.
- On Table 16, write 3ʳᵈ Principal Part + had + been in the margin beside the Past Perfect Tense.
- Time of action of the Verb—it shows an action that had taken place at some definite time in the past.

⑫ Look at Future Perfect Tense: Passive Voice, Table 16.

"I shall/will have been seen," and so forth.

- It is built upon the "Past Participle Stem" (3ʳᵈ Principal Part) + shall/will have + been.
- Note helping Verb "shall/will have." The word "been" makes the action go back to the Subject. That's why it is Passive Voice; the Subject receives the action.
- On Table 16, write 3ʳᵈ Principal Part + shall/will have +been in the margin beside the Future Perfect Tense.
- Time of action of the Verb—it shows an action that will have taken place at some definite time in the future.

After a Super Bowl many years ago, the players were awaiting a parade through a large American city. A sportscaster, interviewing a player as they were waiting, asked, "Is this your first Super Bowl parade?" The player hesitated because he wanted to express an action that would take place at *some definite time in the future*—the Future Perfect Tense—but he didn't know how. Finally he stammered, "This be my first Super Bowl *why not future Tense here?*

parade." It was embarrassing for the young man. If a teacher had begun at the very beginning of Proper Form with him, no doubt he would have said with confidence, "This *will have been* my first Super Bowl Parade."

Now, refer to your notations on Table 16. How many Tenses use the 3rd Principal Part as a building block? That's right, nine. How many tenses are there? That's right, twelve. You only have three left to be formed by the 1st and 2nd Principal Parts. The Present Tense will use the Present Stem. The Past Tense will use the Past Stem. Those are easy! Wow! You only have one to remember and that is the Future Tense—which is "Present Stem + shall/will."

Since you have examined the finished bear, it is time for you to build your own bear. Table 17 offers you a blank paradigm that will assist you in conjugating the Verb, "ride." The Three Principal Parts of ride are "ride—rode—ridden." You can do it!

Table 17. Verb Conjugation Worksheet, using the Verb "ride"

Conjugate the Verb "ride" through all its Tenses, both Active and Passive Voices.

**Active Voice**

| Present Tense | | Present Perfect Tense | |
|---|---|---|---|
| I RIDE | WE RIDE | I HAVE RIDDEN | WE HAVE RIDDEN |
| YOU RIDE | YOU RIDE | YOU HAVE RIDDEN | YOU HAVE RIDDEN |
| HE RIDES | THEY RIDE | HE HAS RIDDEN | THEY HAVE RIDDEN |
| Past Tense | | Past Perfect Tense | |
| I RODE | WE RODE | I HAD RIDDEN | WE HAD RIDDEN |
| YOU RODE | YOU RODE | YOU HAD RIDDEN | |
| HE RODE | THEY RODE | HE HAD RIDDEN | THEY HAD RIDDEN |
| Future Tense | SHALL | Future Perfect Tense | |
| I WILL RIDE | WE WILL RIDE | I WILL HAVE RIDDEN | WE WILL HAVE RIDDEN |
| YOU SHALL RIDE | YOU WILL RIDE | YOU WILL HAVE RIDDEN | |
| HE WILL RIDE | THEY WILL RIDE | HE WILL HAVE RIDDEN | |

THEY WILL HAVE RIDDEN

**Passive Voice**

| Present Tense | Present Perfect Tense *we have been* |
|---|---|
| I am ridden   *we are ridden* | *I have been ridden* |
| *you are ridden* | *you " "* |
| *he is ridden   they are ridden* | *he has been ridden* |
| Past Tense | Past Perfect Tense *They have been* |
| *I was ridden   we were ridden* | *I had been ridden   we "* |
| *you were ridden* | *you "* |
| *He was ridden   They were ridden* | *he "      they "* |
| Future Tense | Future Perfect Tense *we "* |
| *I will be ridden   we ...* | *I will have been ridden* |
| *you will be ridden* | *you "* |
| *He ...      They ...* | *he "      they "* |

Now, carefully compare your Verb conjugation of "ride—rode—ridden" on Table 17 to the conjugation of the Verb "see—saw—seen" in Table 16. Do you see any you have missed? If so, refer to the explanation provided on each of the Tenses. If you think Verb conjugation has been painful, consider all the benefits. It has prepared you to recognize and utilize the Mood, Voice, Tense, Person, and Number of Verbs correctly. Here is a Practice with Verbs Worksheet for you, Table 18, which will hone your skills in identifying the Mood, Voice, Tense, Person, and Number of the Verb. When you have completed the worksheet, Table 18, carefully compare your answers to the Answers for Practice with the Verbs Worksheet, Table 19. Since the Three Principal Parts are vital to Verb Conjugation, Table 20 gives you a long list of the Three Principal Parts of often-used Verbs. *THEY NEED TO BE MEMORIZED.*

Table 18. Practice with Verbs Worksheet

*drive*
*drove*
*driven*

| | Mood | Voice | Tense | Person | Number |
|---|---|---|---|---|---|
| I have driven | IND | A | Pres Perf | 1 ST. | Sing |
| He went | IND | A | Past | 3rd | S |
| They had carried | IND | A | Past Perf | 3rd | P |
| You had been carried | IND | P | Past Perf | 2nd | S/P |
| It has been sung | IND | P | Pres Perf | 3rd | S |

|  | Mood | Voice | Tense | Person | Number |
|---|---|---|---|---|---|
| (you) Sit | IM. | A | Present | 2nd | S/P |
| He ate | IND. | A | Past | 3rd | S |
| They have eaten | IND | A | Past Perf | 3rd | P |
| They have been eaten | IND | P | Past Perf | 3rd | P |
| They are eating | IND | A | Pres. | 3rd | P |
| It has been hidden | IND | P | Pres. P. | 3rd | S |
| I have sat | IND | A | Pres P. | 1st | S |
| You stole | IND | A | P | 2nd | S/P |
| We threw | IND | A | P | 1st | P |
| You will have won | IND | A | F Pre. | 2nd | S/P |
| If I were | SUB | A | P | 1st | S |
| They wrote | IND | A | P | 3rd | P |
| We had written | IND | A | Past Per | 1st | P |
| It is <u>hidden</u> | IND | P | P | 3rd | S |

## Table 19. Answers for Practice with Verbs Worksheet

|  | Mood | Voice | Tense | Person | Number |
|---|---|---|---|---|---|
| I have driven | Indicative | Active | Present Perfect | 1st | Singular |
| He went | Indicative | Active | Past | 3rd | Singular |
| They had carried | Indicative | Active | Past Perfect | 3rd | Plural |
| You had been carried | Indicative | Passive | Past Perfect | 2nd | Singular/Plural |
| It has been sung | Indicative | Passive | Present Perfect | 3rd | Singular |
| Sit | Imperative | Active | Present | 2nd | Singular/Plural |
| He ate | Indicative | Active | Past | 3rd | Singular |
| They have eaten | Indicative | Active | Present Perfect | 3rd | Plural |

|  | Mood | Voice | Tense | Person | Number |
|---|---|---|---|---|---|
| They have been eaten | Indicative | Passive | Present Perfect | 3<sup>rd</sup> | Plural |
| They are eating | Indicative | Active | Present | 3<sup>rd</sup> | Plural |
| It has been hidden | Indicative | Passive | Present Perfect | 3<sup>rd</sup> | Singular |
| I have sat | Indicative | Active | Present Perfect | 1<sup>st</sup> | Singular |
| You stole | Indicative | Active | Past | 2<sup>nd</sup> | Singular/ Plural |
| We threw | Indicative | Active | Past | 1<sup>st</sup> | Plural |
| You will have won | Indicative | Active | Future Perfect | 2<sup>nd</sup> | Singular/ Plural |
| If I were | Subjunctive | Active | Past | 1<sup>st</sup> | Singular |
| They wrote | Indicative | Active | Past | 3<sup>rd</sup> | Plural |
| We had written | Indicative | Active | Past Perfect | 1<sup>st</sup> | Plural |
| It is hidden | Indicative | Passive | Present | 3<sup>rd</sup> | Singular |

Table 20. The Three Principal Parts of often-used Verbs

| Present Stem | CANNOT be used with Helping Verbs (have/has, had, shall/will have) Past Stem | MUST be used with Helping Verbs (have/has, had, shall/will have) Past Participle Stem |
|---|---|---|
| see | saw | seen |
| ride | rode | ridden |
| drink | drank | drunk |
| begin | began | begun |
| eat | ate | eaten |
| go | went | gone |
| break | broke | broken |
| build | built | built |
| burst | burst | burst (not busted) |
| carry | carried | carried |
| come | came | come |
| dig | dug | dug |
| dive | dived, dove | dived |
| be (am) (is) (are) | was/were | been |
| drive | drove | driven |
| fall | fell | fallen |
| fly | flew | flown |
| freeze | froze | frozen |
| give | gave | given |
| grow | grew | grown |
| hang (suspend) | hung | hung |
| hide | hid | hidden |
| hit | hit | hit |

| Present Stem | Past Stem | Past Participle Stem |
| --- | --- | --- |
| know | knew | known |
| lead | led | led |
| lend | lent | lent (not loaned) |
| lie (recline) | lay | lain |
| lay (put or place) | laid | laid |
| ring | rang | rung |
| raise (lift) | raised | raised |
| rise (get up) | rose | risen |
| run | ran | run |
| shake | shook | shaken |
| sing | sang | sung |
| sink | sank | sunk |
| sit (be positioned) | sat | sat |
| set (put or place) | set | set |
| speak | spoke | spoken |
| steal | stole | stolen |
| swim | swam | swum |
| swing | swung | swung |
| tear | tore | torn |
| throw | threw | thrown |
| take | took | taken |

Remember, when you use the Past Stem (2nd Principal Part), you CANNOT use a Helping Verb such as have/has, had, shall/will have. Consider the following incorrect Sentences: "I have saw many movies." "He has ran a business for two years." "The stock market has fell again today." "Jim had ate already." "Susan has went home."

Remember, when you use the Past Participle Stem (3rd Principal Part), you MUST use a Helping Verb such as have/has, had, shall/will have. Consider the following incorrect Sentences: "I seen it in the paper." "I been to that store before," "Clyde drunk too much wine." "I taken it to town."

The Verbs which we have studied so far behave normally and according to pattern. They could be thought of as the "good boy" Verbs. Here come the "bad boys": those which do not behave according to previous pattern and seem to have a radical spirit as they tear up the grammatical countryside. The leader of the pack is a Verb that is called by several names. It is the Verb "to be," "of being," "of existence," and Mrs. McGuillacuddy calls it a "linking Verb." This Verb of existence is made clear by a story in the Old Testament that tells of a prophet who received a message from God. The prophet received the message clearly but then asked the Deity, "What if the people ask who sent me?" The Deity replied, "Tell them I AM has sent you." In other words, "I'm not a god of wood or stone, but the One who exists, who is, who has being." This is the Verb "to be," "of existence," "of being," —a "linking verb." I will refer to this little monster hereafter as the Verb "to be."

This bad boy is not only irregular, but also it causes other grammatical problems throughout the Sentence. *When you use any form of the Verb "to be" (linking verb), the Pronoun which follows must be in the Nominative Case.* This Pronoun is called a Predicate Pronoun. Look under the Nominative Case in your Pronoun Paradigm, Table 6. The Nominative Case is required for Subjects and Predicate Pronouns. You are well aware of what a Subject is; but what is a Predicate Pronoun? *A Predicate Pronoun is a Pronoun that follows any form of the Verb "to be."* Let's examine some Predicate Pronouns!

- This is *he*. (Nominative Case) "He" is a Predicate Pronoun because it follows a form of the Verb "to be." ("Is" is a form of the Verb "to be.")

- The winner will be *she*. (Nominative Case) "She" is a Predicate Pronoun because it follows a form of the Verb "to be." ("Will be" is a form of the Verb "to be.")

- It was *we* who triumphed. "We" is a Predicate Pronoun because it follows a form of the Verb "to be." ("Was" is a form of the Verb "to be.")

*[handwritten margin note: IS WAS to be will be]*

Now, carefully examine the conjugation of the Verb "to be," in the following table, Table 21.

The Three Principal Parts of the Verb "to be" are "am—was—been." Yes, it would be easier if the Verb "to be" were conjugated "I am," "you am," "he am," and so forth, but that is not the case.

*[handwritten: AM   WAS   BEEN]*

Table 21. Conjugation of the Verb "to be": Active Voice only

|  | PERSON | SINGULAR | PLURAL |
|---|---|---|---|
| Present Tense | 1st | I am | We are |
|  | 2nd | You are | You are |
|  | 3rd | He/She/It is | They are |
| Past Tense | 1st | I was | We were |
|  | 2nd | You were | You were |
|  | 3rd | He/She/It was | They were |
| Future Tense | 1st | I shall/will be | We shall/will be |
|  | 2nd | You will be | You will be |
|  | 3rd | He/She/It will be | They will be |
| Present Perfect Tense | 1st | I have been | We have been |
|  | 2nd | You have been | You have been |
|  | 3rd | He/She/It has been | They have been |
| Past Perfect Tense | 1st | I had been | We had been |
|  | 2nd | You had been | You had been |
|  | 3rd | He/She/It had been | They had been |
| Future Perfect Tense | 1st | I shall/will have been | We shall/will have been |
|  | 2nd | You will have been | You will have been |
|  | 3rd | He/She/It will have been | They will have been |

Let's review: Pronouns following the Verb "to be" must be in the Nominative Case. They are called Predicate Pronouns; see Table 6, Personal Pronoun Paradigm. The following exercise, Table 22, will prove to you that you cannot trust sound in matters of Proper Form. Don't even think of guessing! Trusting sound will be disastrous. Use the Nominative Case of the Pronoun following these forms of the Verb "to be," even if you have never "heard" it that way in your entire life.

Complete the exercise Practice with the Verb "to be" on Table 22. Then, check yourself with the Answer Sheet, Table 23. Notice that the Verb "to be" has an *Active Voice only*. The simple reason is that in order "to be" or "to exist" the Subject must be doing it. Otherwise, if you tried to make it Passive Voice, it would be something like, "I am izzed" or "I have been wuzzed."

Table 22. The Verb "to be" Worksheet

1.  This is she/her.

2.  I am he/him who was stranded in the blizzard.

3.  It is I/me; do not be frightened.

4.  It was they/them who robbed the store.

5.  That is he/him, down by the pond.

6.  This is he/him.

7.  It had been we/us who came by the house.

8.  These (men) are they/them.

9.  When the chips are down, it will be he/him who stands by you.

10. The winners will be he/him and she/her.

Table 23. Answers for the Verb "to be" Worksheet
Italicized words are correct.

1.  This is *she*/her.

2.  I am *he*/him who was stranded in the blizzard.

3.  It is *I*/me; do not be frightened.

4.  It was *they*/them who robbed the store.

5. That is *he*/him, down by the pond.

6. This is *he*/him.

7. It had been *we*/us who came by the house.

8. These (men) are *they*/them.

9. When the chips are down, it will be *he*/him who stands by you.

10. The winners will be *he*/him and *she*/her.

You may be gasping in unbelief at this point. Your soul may be crying out, "I've never heard, 'It had been we,' before in my life." Listen to yourself, "I've never heard." Are you trusting sound and every person whom you have ever heard speak or are you trusting simple rule? Sound is an untrustworthy guide; simple rule will never fail you.

Now that you have a good grasp of Predicate Pronouns following "to be," what if the word following a form of the Verb "to be" is an Adjective? When an Adjective follows the Verb "to be," it is called a *Predicate Adjective*.

The soldier was *brave*. Brave = Predicate Adjective.

What if the word following a form of the Verb "to be" is a Noun? When a Noun follows the Verb "to be," it is called a *Predicate Noun*.

It has been a *problem*. Problem = Predicate Noun.

Never use the Objective Case of the Personal Pronoun after the Verb "to be," see Table 6. The Verb "to be" cannot have a Direct Object. Its action is confined to "being." Review the conjugation of the Verb "to be," Table 21. Let's spell it out for clarity.

| | | | |
|---|---|---|---|
| Incorrect: | This is her. | Correct: | This is she. |
| Incorrect: | This is him. | Correct: | This is he. |
| Incorrect: | It was them. | Correct: | It was they. |

Admittedly, it is going against the grain in the real world to use the Nominative Case of the Pronoun after the Verb "to be." For example, if you were to knock on a friend's door you would probably hear a voice from inside saying, "Who is it?" What would be your answer? "It is I," or "It is me." You know which is correct and you know why. Good work!

The Verb "to be" is not the only problem child in the Verb family. There are others: *lie, lay, sit, set*. To understand how to handle these, I am going to introduce two new terms; a *Transitive* Verb and an *Intransitive* Verb.

### *Transitive Verb*:

In Latin, "trans" is a Preposition meaning "across." The action of a Transitive Verb is "moved across" to a Direct Object. Watch these examples of Transitive Verbs:

- Jack *loves* Susan.

  Find the Predicate, and then ask "what or whom." If there is an answer, you have a Direct Object! This time, there is an answer; it is "Susan," which means the Verb is *Transitive*. The action of the Verb, "loves," has been "moved across" to the Direct Object, Susan.

- The car *missed* the tree.

  Find the Predicate, and then ask "what or whom." Is there an answer? Sure, the answer is "tree." It is a Direct Object; hence, the Verb is Transitive. The action of the Verb "missed" has been "moved across" to the Direct Object, "tree."

- The boy *hit* the ball.

  Find the Predicate, and then ask "what or whom." Is there an answer? Sure, it is "ball." The Verb "hit" is Transitive. The action of the Verb "hit" has been "moved across" to the Direct Object, "ball."

### *Intransitive Verb*:

In Latin, "in" is a Preposition meaning "not." When the action of the Verb has *not* been "moved across" to a Direct Object, the Verb is Intransitive. Watch these examples of Intransitive Verbs:

- The dog barked loudly.

  Find the Predicate then ask "what or whom." Is there an answer? No, hence, there is no Direct Object, because no action is being moved across to an Object. The Verb "barked" is In(not) transitive. The action of the Verb "barked" is confined to that Verb only; it is complete within itself.

- I live in Dallas.

    I live "what or whom?" Is there an answer? No, hence, the Verb "live" is Intransitive. The action of the Verb "live" is confined to that Verb only; it is complete within itself.

- He stood in the rain.

    He stood "what or whom?" Is there an answer? No, the Verb "stood" is Intransitive. The action of the Verb "stood" is confined to that Verb only; it is complete within itself.

With the understanding of Transitive and Intransitive Verbs, we can now attack these problem Verbs: lie, lay, sit, set.

"Lie" is an Intransitive Verb meaning "to recline or be positioned." Its Three Principal Parts are lie—lay—lain. It will *never* have a Direct Object. Ask "what or whom" and there will be no answer.

### Lie—Lay—Lain

- I lie (recline) on the couch every night. (Present Tense)
- I lay (reclined) on the couch last night. (Past Tense)
- I have lain (reclined) on the couch all day. (Present Perfect Tense)

"Lay" is a Transitive Verb meaning "to put or place."

Its Three Principal Parts are lay—laid—laid. It will *always* have a Direct Object.

### Lay—Laid—Laid

Underline the Transitive Verbs and circle the Direct Objects that prove the Verbs are Transitive.

- I lay my books on the table every morning. (Present Tense)
- Rover laid his head on my lap. (Past Tense)
- John had laid the lock near the gate. (Past Perfect Tense)

This Verb is often misused in Sentences such as, "I laid down and rested." Laid is a Transitive Verb and must have a Direct Object. There is no Direct Object in this Sentence. The correct Verb would be, "I *lay* down and rested." Lay is an Intransitive Verb in the Past Tense meaning "to recline."

Now, "lie" has a first cousin, "sit" (sit-sat-sat). It also means "to be positioned" and, like "lie," it is always Intransitive; ask "what or whom" and there will be no answer. (Sit-sat-sat will *never* have a Direct Object.)

Sit—Sat—Sat

- He sits (be positioned) in the back row. (Present Tense)

- John sat (be positioned) next to Mary. (Past Tense)

- I have sat (be positioned) there many times myself. (Present Perfect Tense)

Now, "lay" also has a first cousin, "set" (set-set-set). It also means "to put or place" and like "lay," it is always Transitive. (Set-set-set *always* has a Direct Object.)

Set—Set—Set

Underline the Transitive Verbs and circle the Direct Objects that prove the Verbs are Transitive.

- I set the pitcher on the table. (Present Tense)

- They set the furniture last night. (Past Tense)

- John has set many concrete piers (Present Perfect Tense)

Use these simple explanations to guide you as you complete the "lie" and "lay," "sit" and "set," Worksheet, Table 24. Use your knowledge of Transitive and Intransitive Verbs to keep you from guessing.

Table 24. The Verbs "lie" and "lay," "sit" and "set," Worksheet

1. Dr. Jones lays/lies his briefcase on the desk each morning.

2. I lie/lay (present tense) on my couch to watch television.

3. Lie/lay down, Rover!

4. She has lain/laid in the hospital for weeks.

5. Dad lay/laid on the floor last night.

6. Monte lay/laid two thousand bricks last week.

7. I will lie/lay on the soft snow.

8. The accountant had laid/lain in the hammock all day.

9. Here he lies/lays where he once tilled the ground.

10. The hen has lain/laid eggs for many years.

11. Sit/Set down and rest awhile.

12. Jane sat/set by me in the auditorium.

13. Jane sat/set the flowers on the dining table.

14. Please set/sit the vase on the table.

15. Please sit/set by me.

16. John has set/sat by Susan every night this week.

17. You sit/set it there; but then it sets/sits there.

Table 25. Answers for Worksheet with Verbs "lie" and "lay" and "sit" and "set"

Italicized words are correct.

1. Dr. Jones *lays*/lies his briefcase on the desk each morning. ⌐
2. I *lie*/lay (present tense) on my couch to watch television. ⌐
3. *Lie*/lay down, Rover! ⌐
4. She has *lain*/laid in the hospital for weeks. ⌐
5. Dad *lay*/laid on the floor last night. ⌐
6. Monte lay/*laid* two thousand bricks last week. ⌐
7. I will *lie*/lay on the soft snow. ⌐
8. The accountant had laid/*lain* in the hammock all day. ⌐
9. Here he *lies*/lays where he once tilled the ground. ⌐
10. The hen has lain/*laid* eggs for many years. ⌐
11. *Sit*/Set down and rest awhile. ⌐
12. Jane *sat*/set by me in the auditorium. ⌐
13. Jane sat/*set* the flowers on the dining table. ⌐
14. Please *set*/sit the vase on the table. ⌐
15. Please *sit*/set by me. ⌐
16. John has set/*sat* by Susan every night this week. ⌐
17. You sit/*set* it there; but then it sets/*sits* there. ⌐

In case you had any trouble with "lie" and "lay," and "sit" and "set," let's review four of the Sentences that illustrate the proper use of each of these Verbs. This will give you added confidence!

Look at Sentence 5. Dad *lay* on the floor last night.

The Verb means "to recline." Its Three Principal Parts are lie—lay—lain. It is Intransitive (has no Direct Object). Ask the question, "what or whom." There is no answer.

"Sounds simple enough," you say. But how many times have you heard comments such as, "Dad laid on the floor last night," or "He laid down and took a nap." Once again, you cannot trust sound as your guide to Proper Form! Now that you know what is correct, your greatest challenge may be practicing what is correct. You may no longer speak like others around you.

Look at Sentence 10. The hen has *laid* eggs for many years.

The Verb means "to put or place." Its Three Principal Parts are lay—laid—laid. It is Transitive (has a Direct Object). Ask the question "what or whom." There is an answer. It is "eggs."

Look at Sentence 15. Please *sit* by me.

The Verb means "to be positioned." Its Three Principal Parts are sit-sat-sat. It is Intransitive. It has no Direct Object. Ask the question "what or whom." There will be no answer.

Look at Sentence 14. Please *set* the vase on the table.

The Verb means "to put or place." Its Three Principal Parts are set—set—set. It is Transitive. Ask the question "what or whom." There is an answer. It is "vase."

The same grandmother who worked to learn the Three Principal Parts of Verbs had a favorite Sentence that reminded her of the correct usage of "Sit and Set." It is Sentence 17.

"You *set* (put or place) it there; then it *sits* (is positioned) there."

Does this make sense to you? Sure it does. Good job!

We have not reached Participles yet, but while we are in the neighborhood, let's take a quick peek at them. The same rules apply to Participles as apply to Verbs.

The Verb lie—lay—lain has a Participle which is "lying."

The man, *lying* (reclining) on the pavement, is injured.

The Participle has no Object; hence, it is Intransitive: (like lie—lay—lain).

The Verb lay—laid—laid has a Participle which is "laying."

The man, *laying* (placing) bricks, is my dad.

The Participle has an Object; hence, it is Transitive; (like lay—laid—laid).

Just for fun, tell me what the Object of the Participle is! Sure, it is "bricks."

## LET'S VISIT

How are you doing thus far? Whether you realize it or not, you have come through the deepest waters of Proper Form: Nouns, Pronouns, and Verbs. Pronouns and Verbs have a multiplicity of forms, and you have learned the rules that allow you to choose the correct form. You have forsaken "sounds right" as a guideline and have left "guesswork" in your rear view mirror. Congratulations!

At this point, it is important to relax and to learn, and if possible, to enjoy it. The guidelines for the future are to retain your poise and to learn at a comfortable, unrushed tempo. You can always stop and start again tomorrow. I suggest that you make these rest stops at the end of each chapter.

# Chapter 5

## Focusing on Adjectives and Adverbs

An *Adjective* is a word that describes a Noun (limits, defines, identifies, modifies ala Mrs. McGuillacuddy) by telling three things: *Which one, What kind, or How many.*

The *pink* (which one) flower is a rose.

(See how the Adjective "pink" describes the Noun "flower"?)

The *tender* (what kind) steak costs more.

(See how the Adjective "tender" describes the Noun "steak"?)

*Seven* (how many) scholars worked on the project.

(See how the Adjective "seven" describes the Noun, "scholars"?)

Now, in the Sentences above, draw a line from the Adjective to the Noun it describes (or modifies).

In English, Adjectives can describe Nouns as shown above (Positive Degree). But oftentimes our need to describe a Noun extends to the place where one Noun's description must be compared to another Noun's description (Comparative Degree). And then, we may be required to describe a Noun in relation to several other Nouns (Superlative Degree). Because of this, English has what is called *Comparison of Adjectives.* There are three "Degrees" in the Comparison of Adjectives Paradigm. See Table 26.

Table 26. Comparison of Adjectives Paradigm

| Positive Degree | Comparative Degree | Superlative Degree |
|---|---|---|
| Describing One | Comparing Two | Comparing Three or More |
| PURE | PURER | PUREST |
| PRETTY | PRETTIER | PRETTIEST |
| POWERFUL | MORE POWERFUL | MOST POWERFUL |
| BEAUTIFUL | MORE BEAUTIFUL | MOST BEAUTIFUL |
| SOFT | SOFTER | SOFTEST |
| SWEET | SWEETER | SWEETEST |
| FAST | FASTER | FASTEST |
| Mom is a *fast* driver. | Dad is a *faster* driver than Mom. | Granddad is the *fastest* driver in the family. |

Take a look at the Adjective, soft—softer—softest, as it describes a Noun.

Good Value is *soft* tissue. (Positive Degree)

Fluffy Cloud is *softer* tissue than Good Value tissue. (Comparative Degree)

Ultra Puff is the *softest* tissue on the market. (Superlative Degree)

Notice that the degrees are formed by adding "—ER" and "—EST" in most cases. Sometimes "more" or "most" is needed to complete the paradigm. Be careful never to combine "more" or "most" with words that end in "—ER" or "—EST" (more purer, most sweetest, and so forth).

Now, make a Sentence using the Positive, Comparative, and Superlative degrees of any Adjective.

1. Positive Degree = *Sally is a sweet girl.*
2. Comparative Degree = *Sally is sweeter than Sue.*
3. Superlative Degree = *Sally is the sweetest girl in OK.*

I knew you could do it!

There are other Adjectives which are called "irregular" because they do not use "—ER" or "—EST"—or "more" or "most" to form the Comparative and Superlative Degrees. In fact, they have completely different words to express these degrees.

| Positive Degree | Comparative Degree | Superlative Degree |
|---|---|---|
| GOOD | BETTER | BEST |
| BAD | WORSE | WORST |

- This is *good* pecan pie. (Positive Degree)
- The coconut pie is *better* than the pecan pie. (Comparative Degree)
- The buttermilk pie is the *best* pie on the shelf. (Superlative Degree)

Note: "Good" is the Positive Degree of the Adjective. "Well" is the Positive Degree of the Adverb.

Jack is a good singer. (Good = Positive Degree of the Adjective.) (See how "good" describes the Noun, "singer"?)

Jack sings well. (Well = Positive Degree of the Adverb.) (See how "well" describes the Verb, "sings"?)

You learned in Chapter 1 that Adjectives describe Nouns and Adverbs describe Verbs. This bit of knowledge will be key as we go further into the study of Adjectives and Adverbs.

As with Verbs, there are some Adjectives which present problems. Once we isolate them, they are not so complex after all. Consider the following:

| Positive Degree | Comparative Degree | Superlative Degree |
|---|---|---|
| LITTLE | LESS | LEAST |

This Adjective is used when Nouns *are not* quantifiable (can't be counted).

- Jack put out *little* effort on the test. (You can't count effort.)
- Jim put out *less* effort than Jack. (You can't count effort.)
- Paul put out the *least* effort of anyone in the class. (You can't count effort.)

| Positive Degree | Comparative Degree | Superlative Degree |
|---|---|---|
| FEW | FEWER | FEWEST |

This Adjective is used when Nouns *are* quantifiable (can be counted).

- There were *few* casualties in the war this week. (You can count casualties.)

- There were *fewer* casualties in the war this week than last week. (You can count casualties.)

- There were the *fewest* casualties in the war of any week since the fighting began. (You can count casualties.)

Errors are often made on food labels, stating facts such as, "Our light product has 250 less calories than our original brand." Can you count calories? Sure. They are quantifiable so you need to use few-fewer-fewest. The correct Sentence should read, "Our light product has 250 fewer calories than our original brand." The same is true for a retailer whose check-out sign reads, incorrectly, "10 items or less." Can you count items? Certainly. It should read, "Ten items or fewer." There was a recent cartoon that showed a check-out line with only a few people in it. A sign above the line read, "Check-out line for English majors." A smaller sign, in bold font read, "Ten items or fewer." Isn't it great to learn and to have fun at the same time?

## ADJECTIVES WHICH CANNOT BE COMPARED.

There are some Adjectives which have no Comparative or Superlative Degrees. They can't be compared; they are absolutes. Here are a few: *round, empty, unique, equal*. A round moon cannot be rounder. An empty gas tank cannot be emptier or emptiest. A unique (one of a kind) person cannot be "most unique." Many student essays begin with, "My granddad is the most unique man in the world." Incorrect! Granddad could be the most admirable man in the world, but he could not be the most unique. And finally, equal. Political rhetoric often says, "We need a tax code that is more equal." Or "The United States has the most equal tax code in the world." Incorrect! And you know why!

I often read from newspapers to let the students see that the media cannot always be trusted to utilize Proper Form. Here are a few choice examples dealing with degrees of the Adjective:

- "The Detroit, Michigan Company was the 'lower' of three bidders for the job." What is wrong here?  *lowest*

- "There are three, four, or five top teams and there is only one way to determine who the 'better' team is." What's wrong here?  *best*

- "In an MRI machine, the more powerful the magnet, the 'more clearer' the images." What's wrong here?

You are doing well! I know that you spotted each error quickly.

Now let's look at the Comparison of Adverbs. The same, simple principles apply. By definition, an *Adverb* is a word that describes (modifies) a Verb by telling three things: *How, When,* or *Where.*

The musician practices *diligently*. (Tells how)

(See how the Adverb "diligently" describes the Verb "practices"?)

The chairman of the board arrives *early* for each meeting. (Tells when)

(See how the Adverb "early" describes the Verb "arrives"?)

The marketing department sets the standard high for the commercials. (Tells where)

(See how the Adverb "high" describes the Verb "sets"?)

Now, in the three Sentences above, draw a line from the Adverb to the Verb it describes (or modifies).

The Three Degrees Principle applies not only to the Adjective, but also to the Adverb.

Table 27. Comparison of Adverbs Paradigm

| Positive Degree | Comparative Degree | Superlative Degree |
|---|---|---|
| Describing One | Comparing Two | Comparing Three or More |
| WELL | BETTER | BEST |
| SLOW | SLOWER | SLOWEST |
| SOON | SOONER | SOONEST |
| BEAUTIFULLY | MORE BEAUTIFULLY | MOST BEAUTIFULLY |
| SWEETLY | MORE SWEETLY | MOST SWEETLY |
| FAST | FASTER | FASTEST |
| Mom drives *fast*. | Dad drives *faster* than Mom. | Granddad drives the *fastest* of anyone in the family. |

Fast can also be an Adjective if it modifies a Noun. "Mom is a *fast* driver." Refer to Table 26, Comparison of Adjectives Paradigm. In Table 27, above, "fast" is an Adverb describing the Verb "drives." "Mom drives fast." Do you see how "fast" can be either an Adjective or an Adverb according to the word it describes?

Like Adjectives, there are also Adverbs which cannot be compared. Here are a few: *always, completely, immediately, and perfectly*. There is no "more always," or "most always." This reminds me of the old wedding song of years past, "I'll be loving you, always."

The Subject was covered "completely." There is no "more completely" or "most completely." Jack responded "immediately." There is no "more immediately" or "most immediately." Likewise, Emily played the clarinet solo "perfectly." There is no "more perfectly" or "most perfectly."

Before finishing Adjectives and Adverbs, (since you know what each is and how each is used) let's address a sticky little problem. That problem is the similarity between the irregular Adjective, good—better—best; and the irregular Adverb, well—better—best. My first teaching job was in a mid-size Texas town. Our football coach would stand in Pep Assembly each week and say, "Our boys hit real good." Of course, "good" is an Adjective and as such cannot describe (modify) the Verb "hit"—that's an Adverb's work. ("I caught that one," you might say.) Great! But we seem to have defined ourselves into a corner here. How so? We have chiseled in stone the rule, "Adverbs describe (modify) Verbs." With the strict adherence to that rule, let's proceed. Is it correct to say, "The pie tastes well?" "Taste" is surely a Verb and "well" is the Positive Degree of the Adverb. We can't go around saying that. Here is the wiggle out of it. _Verbs of the five senses: see, hear, smell, feel, and taste may be followed by the Adjective, good_. The pie tastes good. The cake smells good. I feel good (or well). I hear good (or well). I see good (or well). I (can) smell good (or well).

# Chapter 6

## Focusing on Prepositions, Conjunctions, and Interjections

Let's get *Interjections* out of the way; they are the easiest Part of Speech to learn. An *Interjection* is simply a word that shows strong feeling.

> *Wow*! This is great steak.
>
> *Look out*! A train is coming.
>
> *Help!* The child fell into the water.

Note: An exclamation point follows an Interjection and the word following the Interjection is always capitalized.

Now, to the discussion of *Prepositions* and *Conjunctions.* These Parts of Speech are "connectors"—just as Adjectives and Adverbs are "describers."

A *Preposition* is a word that connects *Words* and *Phrases* to the rest of the Sentence. (A Phrase is a group of words which has neither Subject nor Predicate and does not make sense.) You may remember Phrase as being a member of The Big Three; Sentence, Clause, and Phrase in Chapter I. You would do well to reread the definitions of Sentence, Clause, and Phrase!

Here are some often-used Prepositions: About, above, beneath, beside, behind, into, upon, inside, outside, with, within, among, between, around, and of. But the most famous reindeer of all is the Preposition "like." We shall take a close look at the Preposition "like" later.

A student once told me that her high school English teacher defined a Preposition as "anything a squirrel can do to a tree." At first, that didn't seem scholarly enough, and I still don't give credit on tests for it, but that about covers it. A squirrel can be up a tree, under a tree, around a tree, behind a tree, and so forth. More importantly, remember that Prepositions connect Words and Phrases to the rest of the Sentence.

Look how Prepositions can connect *Words* in the Sentences below. I shall begin, and you will complete this exercise:

1. The border *of* Oklahoma is crooked. ("Of" connects Oklahoma and border.)

2. The boy left *with* his dad. ("With" connects dad and left.)

3. The main office is *in* Dallas. ("In" connects Dallas and office.)

4. The girl walked *into* the room. ("Into" connects ___girl___ and ___room___.)

5. Corn syrup tastes *like* honey. ("Like" connects ___c. syrup___ and ___honey___.)

6. John walked *beside* Mary. ("Beside" connects ___John___ and ___Mary___.)

7. The pact was made *among* the three friends. ("Among" connects ___pact___ and ___friends___.)

8. Another pact was made *between* the two friends. ("Between" connects ___pact___ and ___friends___.)

The above examples show how Prepositions can connect *Words*. Prepositions can also connect *Phrases*. Watch how Prepositions connect the following Phrases:

1. I sank *like a rock plunging to the bottom*. (Preposition = like)

2. I saw the animal *with a long, green, slimy-looking tail*. (Preposition = with)

3. He reminded me *of a bird fluttering to the ground*. (Preposition = of)

4. The minister encouraged me *by reminding me of my success*. (Preposition = by)

Since a Preposition is a connector, it does not fit well at the end of a Sentence. It doesn't connect anything in this position. It is not considered unpardonable, nowadays, to end a Sentence with a Preposition. However, in formal writing or speaking, it resembles a tattered thread on a tuxedo.

Technically, the following Sentences are incorrect because they end with Prepositions:

1. Oklahoma City is where I come *from*.

2. Look what I have to put up *with*.

3. It is the room I walked *into*.

4. The game was the biggest I've ever played *in*.

5. Susan is the one Dad had trouble *with*.

6. She is the happiest person I've been *around*.

7. Where are you *at*?

In short, a Preposition is not a good word to end a Sentence *with*. Whoops!

Before leaving Prepositions, let's examine the most famous reindeer of all, "like." You may have heard of "hate speech." It is bad. "Like" speech also makes the skin crawl. What is "like" speech? Here is a direct quotation from a graduating senior who was asked to comment on the outcome of a trial:

"I thought like, who do they pay off because all of the jurors were like, 'he's not guilty,' but I was like, 'I agree with them.'"

Mercy! That is an example of "like" speech and it tells the whole world in an instant that the speaker has no idea how a Preposition functions. It may sound cool, but it is condemning. Here are some examples of college students utilizing "like" speech:

- "I was like, 'Are you going to the game?'"

- "He was like, 'I don't think I am.'"

- "I was like, 'This is the last game of the season.'"

- "He was like, 'You really think I ought to go?'"

Now that this condemnation of current colloquialism has been addressed, let's proceed in our rational discussion of connectors. In the world of connectors, Prepositions remain in second place. They are sometimes called "weak connectors" because they can connect Words and Phrases, only.

Conjunctions are the "strong connectors." They can join Words, Phrases, and Clauses. By definition, a *Conjunction* is a word that can be used to connect *Words, Phrases,* and *Clauses* to the rest of the Sentence.

Years ago there was a cigarette tagline that said, "Winston tastes good, like a cigarette should." Problem: "like" is a Preposition and "cigarette should" constitutes a Clause (Subject + Predicate). A Preposition is not strong enough to pull a heavy Clause. That is the work of the powerful Conjunction. Aye, there's the rub! Often people try to connect and to pull a heavy Clause (Subject and Predicate) with a little ole weak Preposition. The weak Preposition simply cannot pull it. Although English teachers whined throughout the decade, the tagline was not changed. It should have read, "Winston tastes good *as* a cigarette should." "As" is a big, bold Conjunction.

I recall one of the commentators on Monday Night Football. He would say, "I tell it like it is." Being highly educated, he no doubt knew better. What he did not realize was the strength of the virus he was spreading that would attack Proper Form. For decades, people in every echelon of society proudly proclaimed, "I tell it like it is." Students make this error on papers and in conversation until they are told that "it" is a Subject and "is" functions as a Predicate; which constitutes a Clause. "Like" is a Preposition. It cannot pull a heavy Clause. It should read, "I tell it *as* it is." There are many other examples of the use of the weak connector (Preposition) when a strong connector (Conjunction) is needed. Look at this Sentence:

"I feel like I am going to faint."

Obviously, "I am going to faint" is a Clause. See the Subject and Predicate? "Like" can't pull it; therefore, the Conjunction "*as if*" should be used. "I feel *as if* I am going to faint."

A young man from eastern Oklahoma who lived on a ranch told me how he kept Prepositions and Conjunctions separate. He said he had a small pickup truck with which he did small jobs. Pickup started with a "P." It was his weak connector (like a Preposition). But, he continued that when he had a heavy load, such as a big, round bale of hay, he had a two-and-a-half ton truck that he could "hook up," which corresponded to the heavy-hauling Conjunction. To give due credit, the student never got the two connectors (Preposition and Conjunction) confused.

Do you remember the "Grammar Rock" kids' show that used to be on TV? A student taped the entire series and brought it to class. Although each Part of Speech has its own melody and jingle, the Conjunction lyrics are my favorite. "Conjunction Junction, What's your function? Hookin' up Words, and Phrases and Clauses. *And, but, or* will take you oh so far." That says it well! And that brings up the need to list a few Conjunctions. Of course, as the lyrics say, "and," "but," and "or" are frequently used. But here are some more Conjunctions: as, as if, because, inasmuch, till, so, so that, after, since, unless, before, although, then, whenever, while, moreover, however. Since you understand the difference between the two connectors, Prepositions and Conjunctions, let's examine the heavy haulers closely.

Conjunctions are separated into three types: Coordinate, Correlative, and Subordinate. Take these slowly. Retain your poise. You've already learned more difficult things than this.

1. The *Coordinate Conjunction* connects Sentence elements of equal value. (It coordinates.) It almost defines itself.

   - The dog *and* the cat played together. (See the Sentence elements of equal value?)

   - John *or* Mary will have to go. (See the Sentence elements of equal value?)

   - Susan worked every day *and* studied every night. (See the Sentence elements of equal value?)

   - He hurried, *but* he did not catch the train. (See the Sentence elements of equal value?)

2. The *Correlative Conjunction* connects Sentence elements of equal value—but it comes in pairs. (It correlates.) It almost defines itself.

   - *Not only* the man *but also* his dog was ill-tempered. If you have a "not only"—you must have a "but also." See how these twin Conjunctions correlate man and dog?

   - Neither the President *nor* the Vice President knew the answer. If you have a "neither," you must have a "nor." See how these twin conjunctions correlate President and Vice President?

   - Either the apple or cinnamon will be acceptable. If you have an "either," you must have an "or." See how these twin

Conjunctions correlate apple and cinnamon?

- Both the coach and the players were overjoyed. If you have a "both," you must have an "and." See how these twin Conjunctions correlate coach and players?

Finally, here is the most challenging of the three types of Conjunctions. (Pretend a charcoal steak and baked potato are awaiting you after learning the Subordinate Conjunction.) My next book will be about the relationship of food and academic progress. There must be a correlation!

3. The *Subordinate Conjunction* is used when one idea is dependent upon another. The word "subordinate" comes from the Latin "sub," which means "under" and "ate," the suffix, which means "process of." Hence, it is a Conjunction that causes one Clause to be placed under the other, subordinating one Clause to the other. Take a look at this Sentence:

"Although it is old, the car is beautiful."

See the two Clauses? (The two groups of words that have a Subject and a Predicate) The one Clause that doesn't make sense— "Although it is old"—depends on the other Clause for its meaning. Therefore, it is called a *Dependent Clause.* The one that makes sense—and needs nothing else—is called an *Independent Clause.* "The car is beautiful" is an Independent Clause and could stand alone as a Sentence.

Look at these Sentences which have Dependent Clauses and Independent Clauses:

- *Although* the rains came, the farmers continued to plow.

   "Although" is a subordinating Conjunction because it makes the first Clause dependent on the second Clause for its meaning. If you removed "Although," you would have another Independent Clause. "The rains came" could stand alone as a Sentence. So, this is the function of the Subordinating Conjunction. It subordinates one Clause (the Dependent Clause) to the other (the Independent Clause).

- *Because* the missionary carried food, the natives welcomed him.

  "Because" makes that Clause dependent—it subordinates it. "Because" is a Subordinate Conjunction.

- *Whenever* my family gathers, there is much laughter.

  "Whenever" makes that Clause dependent—it subordinates it. "Whenever" is a Subordinate Conjunction.

- *When* crime increased, the police began surveillance.

  "When" makes that Clause dependent—it subordinates it. "When" is a Subordinate Conjunction.

- I've decided to stay home, *since* it is snowing outside.

  "Since" makes that Clause dependent—it subordinates it. "Since" is a Subordinate Conjunction.

- *Unless* the renter pays his rent, he will be evicted.

  "Unless" makes that Clause dependent—it subordinates it. "Unless" is a Subordinate Conjunction.

Do you see how the Subordinate Conjunction in each of these Sentences "subordinates" one Clause (the Dependent Clause) to the other (the Independent Clause)? Sure you do. Good work.

The bottom line on these connectors is that Prepositions can connect *Words and Phrases* only, while Conjunctions can connect *Words, Phrases, and Clauses.*

# Chapter 7

## Focusing on Verbals (Gerunds, Participles, and Infinitives)

At last, here comes the Grand Finale of Proper Form. All the elemental themes have been played and now the symphony comes together in one grandiose swelling, intermingling and mixing in ways not realized heretofore. The names of the contributing movements are Gerund, Participle, and Infinitive. They are called Verbals because each is constructed by using a Verb form.

Let's begin with the simplest, the *Gerund*. A Gerund is a Verb form that ends in "—ing" but that functions as a Noun. My tiny Latin Professor said one morning, "Oh, Gerunds are easy; they are part Verb and part Noun—like a Verb they show action, but like a Noun they become Subjects, Direct Objects, Indirect Objects, and Objects of Prepositions. Any place you can use a Noun; you can use a Gerund."

The light slowly began to dawn upon me. May it dawn upon you, too! You can always remember that Gerunds are used as Nouns because of the "N" in GERUND. Circle the "N" in Gerund and you will never be confused.

Table 28. Gerund Paradigm

| VERBS | GERUNDS |
|-------|---------|
|       | **Verb form + "-ing" used as a Noun** |
| Jump  | Jumping |
| Run   | Running |
| Keep  | Keeping |
| See   | Seeing  |
| Ride  | Riding  |

As you can see, Gerunds are formed by taking the *Present Stem of the Verb and adding "—ing."* Aren't you glad you know all about Verbs? Now, let's see how Gerunds function as Nouns.

First, Gerunds can be used as Subjects: (like Nouns).

1. <u>*Learning* can be exciting</u>. "Learn" (Verb form) plus "—ing" = learning; a Gerund. See how this Gerund is used as the Subject?

    See how the Gerund "learning" is half Verb (action) and half Noun because it is used as the Subject?

2. *Smoking* may be dangerous to your health. "Smoke" (Verb form) plus "—ing" = smoking; a Gerund.

    See how the Gerund "smoking" is half Verb (action) and half Noun because it is used as the Subject?

3. *Seeing* is believing. "See" (Verb form) plus "—ing" = seeing; a Gerund.

    See how the Gerund "seeing" is half Verb (action) and half Noun because it is used as the Subject?

4. *Coming* home is a joy. "Come" (Verb form) plus "—ing" = coming; a Gerund.

    See how the Gerund "coming" is half Verb (action) and half Noun because it is used as the Subject?

5. *Riding* horses makes me happy. "Ride" (Verb form) plus "—ing" = riding; a Gerund.

See how the Gerund "riding" is half Verb (action) and half Noun because it is used as the Subject?

Second, Gerunds can be used as Direct Objects: (like Nouns).

1. Lillian loved (what?) *swimming*.

    If the Sentence read, "Lillian loved candy," "candy" would be an old-fashioned Noun used as a Direct Object. "Swimming" is a Gerund. Swimming is also a Direct Object. See how "swimming" is half Verb (action) and half Noun because it is used as a Direct Object? Use this reasoning on Sentences 2—5.

2. Do you remember (what?) *finding* this picture? (The Gerund "finding" is the Direct Object.)

3. In high school, Jack discovered (what?) *running*. (The Gerund "running" is the Direct Object.)

4. In the speech, the coach praised (what?) *exercising*. (The Gerund "exercising" is the Direct Object.)

5. In college, she loved (what?) *dancing*. (The Gerund "dancing" is the Direct Object.)

    Any way you can use a Noun, you can use a Gerund.

Third, Gerunds can be used as Indirect Objects (infrequently however): (like Nouns).

Jack gave *singing* the credit for his success.

Singing functions as an Indirect Object here. It answers the question, "to whom or for whom"—"credit" would be the Direct Object.

Fourth, Gerunds can be used as *Objects of Prepositions*. Before continuing with some clear examples of how a Gerund can be used as the Object of a Preposition, let's punch the refresh button and review how an old-fashioned Noun is used as an Object of a Preposition.

"The boy hit the ball with a *bat*."

"With" is a Preposition. "Bat" is an old-fashioned Noun and is the Object of the Preposition "with."

In the Sentences below, Objects of the Preposition are not old-fashioned Nouns. They are Gerunds; part Verb and part Noun.

1. *With the coming* of spring, spirits soar.

   See how "with" is a Preposition and "coming" is the Object of that Preposition? ("Coming" is a Gerund; come + ing.)

2. He has succeeded *in carrying* the water to the troops.

   See how "in" is a Preposition and "carrying" is the Object of that Preposition? ("Carrying" is a Gerund; carry + ing.)

3. Johnny dreamed *of climbing* the corporate ladder.

   See how "of" is a Preposition and "climbing" is the Object of that Preposition? ("Climbing" is a Gerund; climb + ing.)

4. His body was invigorated *by running.*

   See how "by" is a Preposition and "running" is the Object of that Preposition?

   ("Running" is a Gerund; run + ning.)

5. There is a way *of knowing* the truth.

   See how "of" is a Preposition and "knowing" is the Object of that Preposition? ("Knowing" is a Gerund; know + ing.)

Fifth, Gerunds can be used as Predicate Nouns. These are the Nouns that follow the Verb "to be." "Is," "was," "will be," "has been," "had been," and "shall/will have been" are forms of the Verb "to be." (See Table 21.) A Noun that follows any of these Verb forms will be a Predicate Noun. The example given earlier for the Predicate Noun was, "It has been a problem." "Has been" is a form of the Verb "to be" and "problem" is the Noun that follows. Hence, "problem" is a Predicate Noun. Now, Gerunds (half Verb and half Noun) can be used in the same way as old-fashioned Nouns. Let's look at one other example of an old-fashioned Noun's being used as a Predicate Noun. Then, I shall show you how a Gerund (half Verb and half Noun) can also be used as a Predicate Noun.

"He is the man."

"Is" is a form of the Verb "to be" and "man" is the Predicate Noun. A half Verb—half Noun (Gerund) may also follow the Verb "to be" and serve as a Predicate Noun. Look at these examples of a Gerund serving as a Predicate Noun.

1. His passion *will be studying*. (Gerund used as a Predicate Noun after the Verb "to be")

2. Our interest *is learning*. (Gerund used as a Predicate Noun after the Verb "to be")

3. John's dream *was flying*. (Gerund used as a Predicate Noun after the Verb "to be")

4. Their occupation *has been loafing*. (Gerund used as a Predicate Noun after the Verb "to be")

Now, let's spotlight the area where many errors are made in the use of Gerunds and that is the failure to use a *Possessive Pronoun* before the Gerund. Take time to look at your Pronoun Paradigm, Table 7, and you will see that the *Possessive Case* is used to "show ownership," but also, it is used "before a Gerund." When the Gerund is not recognized, writers/speakers fail to use the Possessive Pronoun in front of it.

I have a cartoon of a woman complaining to her husband. She says, "What's the use of 'me' losing two pounds if nobody notices?" As you know, "losing" is a Gerund, in fact, it is a Gerund used as an Object of the Preposition "of" (of losing). Hence, the Sentence should read, "What's the use of *my* losing two pounds if nobody notices?" The rule cannot be expressed any more succinctly than, *Use the Possessive Pronoun before the Gerund*. Let's put this knowledge into practice. Complete Table 29, Gerund Worksheet and compare your answers to Table 30, Answers to Gerund Worksheet.

Table 29. Gerund Worksheet

Underline the Gerund and circle the correct Pronoun:

1. I appreciate him/his (teaching) me.

2. Them/Their flying to Dallas saved the company money.

3. Mom enjoyed us/our coming home.

4. The pastor appreciated them/their cooking at camp.

5. Do you mind me/my calling the President?

6. Would you have imagined him/his being an executive? (The Verb "to be" + "—ing" = being; a Gerund.)

7. The colonel appreciated you/<u>your</u> <u>carrying</u> the flag.

8. Thank you for preparing for me/<u>my</u> <u>coming</u> to the boardroom.

9. There is a reason for him/<u>his</u> <u>arriving</u> late.

10. I was pleased by them/<u>their</u> <u>bringing</u> prepared budgets.

Table 30. Answers for Gerund Worksheet

Italicized words are correct

1. I appreciate him/*his* teaching me.

2. Them/*Their* flying to Dallas saved the company money.

3. Mom enjoyed us/*our* coming home.

4. The pastor appreciated them/*their* cooking at camp.

5. Do you mind me/*my* calling the President?

6. Would you have imagined him/*his* being an executive? (The Verb "to be" + "-ing" = being; a Gerund.)

7. The colonel appreciated you/*your* carrying the flag.

8. Thank you for preparing for me/*my* coming to the boardroom.

9. There is a reason for him/*his* arriving late.

10. I was pleased by them/*their* bringing prepared budgets.

If a Noun comes before a Gerund, the Noun also must be in the Possessive Case.

"*Jerry's* coming home thrilled us." (Jerry's = Possessive Case)

The second contributing theme in the Grand Finale is the Participle. A <u>P(a)rticiple is a Verb form that functions as an Adjective</u> (just as the <u>Gerund is a Verb form that functions as a Noun</u>). You can always remember that a Participle is an Adjective because of the "A" in P<u>A</u>RTICIPLE. Cheap trick, but it works. Circle the "A" in Participle and you will never be confused. Again, we have two genetic inputs into a Participle—the Verb and the Adjective. My Latin Professor went on to say, "Participles are also easy; they are part Verb and part Adjective. As a Verb, they show action, but as an Adjective, they tell 'which one,' 'what kind,' or 'how many' as they describe Nouns."

Once again, there is no hurry. Draw upon your knowledge of Verbs and Adjectives to see if you can understand how a word could be "part Verb and part Adjective"; a Participle.

1.  The woman, *carrying* the umbrella, looked happy.

    > Although "carrying" is a Verb form ending in "—ing," it is not a Gerund this time. It is a Participle because it describes the Noun "woman." It tells "which woman" (the one carrying the umbrella) like an Adjective, but it also shows action like a Verb. A Participle is half Verb and half Adjective. It shows action as a Verb does while describing the woman (the one carrying the umbrella) as an Adjective does.

2.  The criminal, *falling* to his knees, surrendered.

    > "Falling" is a Participle. It is part Verb and part Adjective. See how "falling" shows action as a Verb does while describing the criminal (the one falling to the knees) as an Adjective does?

3.  The bottle, *carried* by the river, plopped into the ocean.

    > "Carried" is a Participle. It is part Verb and part Adjective. See how "carried" shows action as a Verb does while describing bottle as an Adjective does? It tells which bottle (the one carried by the river).

Remember when you read about the Three Principal Parts of the Verb and the last one had a mystifying name called a "Past Participle"? And I wrote in so many words, "We'll understand it better by and by." Now is the time. "Carried" is a Past Participle. Its action takes place in the past as opposed to "carrying" which takes place in the present and is a Present Participle. Every third Principal Part of a Verb is the Past Participle. This is where the third Principal Part gets its name. In Verb conjugation, we used the Past Participle Stem (Third Principal Part) as the basis for nine of the twelve Tenses in the conjugational scheme.

Now, just for fun, let's analyze Sentence number one. You'll be surprised at how much you know!

"The woman, *carrying* the umbrella, looked happy."

Knowing what you know about conjugating Verbs, in what *Tense* is the Participle "carrying"? Present. You are correct. Now, knowing what you know about Verb conjugation, in what *Voice* is this Participle? Active. You are correct. "Carrying" is a *Present Active Participle*.

Keep it up! Look at the Participle in Sentence number three—"carried."

"The bottle, *carried* by the river, plopped into the ocean."

Knowing what you know about conjugating Verbs, in what *Tense* is the Participle "carried"? Past. You are correct. Now, knowing what you know about Verb conjugation, in what *Voice* is this Participle? Passive. You are correct. This is a *Past Passive Participle.* Now you can "talk the talk." Good job!

While we are here, if you had a Sentence that read, "The bottle, *having been carried* by the river, plopped into the ocean," it would be a Perfect Passive Participle because it uses the helping Verb of the Present Perfect Tense—"have." How about that!

Isn't it great to be able to draw upon your background in Proper Form? Now, let's press on and compare some old-fashioned Adjectives with Participles and see exactly how they differ. This will allow you to conquer Participles.

1. The *cold* rain covered my windshield. (Cold = old-fashioned Adjective describing "rain.")

2. The *freezing* rain covered my windshield. (Present Stem of the Verb "freeze" + "—ing" = Participle.) See how "freezing," the Participle, describes the Noun "rain," but "freezing" has an element of action in it. That's the genetic input of the Verb! A Participle is part Verb and part Adjective.

3. I like to watch the *tall* waves. (Tall = old-fashioned Adjective describing "waves.")

4. I like to watch the *rolling* waves. (Present Stem of the Verb "roll" + "—ing" = Participle.) See how "rolling," the Participle, describes the Noun "waves," while it also contributes an element of action. That's the genetic input of the Verb! A Participle is Part Verb and Part Adjective.

Have you heard of a dangling Participle? They are also correctly called *misplaced modifiers*. A dangling Participle is best defined by example:

"The woman saw the monkey carrying her purse."

By the placement of the Participle "carrying" in this Sentence, a reader can't tell if it is a woman carrying her purse or a female monkey carrying her purse. In other words, the Participle "carrying" dangles and the reader can't tell where it fits. It is, indeed, a misplaced modifier.

Now here is a big question that may be on your mind: If a Gerund is a Verb form ending in "—ing" and the Present Participle is a Verb form ending in "—ing," how can you tell them apart? (It is important to be able to do so because you do not want to use a Possessive Pronoun in front of a Participle.) Here's how. Remember a Participle is used as an Adjective. (It's half Verb and half Adjective.) Remember a Gerund is used as a Noun. (It's half Verb and half Noun.)

1. He saw *me*/my sitting on the ground.

> He saw what or whom?—He saw "me." "Me" is the Direct Object. "Sitting" is a Participle serving as an Adjective describing "me." Hence, you would use the Personal Pronoun in the Objective Case "Me." "He saw *me* sitting on the ground."

2. He complained of me/*my* sitting on the ground.

> Here you have a Preposition, "of"—"of sitting." "Sitting" is a Gerund, because it is used as the Object of a Preposition (like a Noun). Hence, you would use the Personal Pronoun in the Possessive Case. "He complained of *my* sitting on the ground."

The last contributing theme to the Grand Finale of Proper Form is the Infinitive. An *Infinitive* is a Verb form in its Present Stem preceded by the word "to." Oftentimes, the word "to" is used as a Preposition which connects a Noun to the rest of the Sentence.

I am going to town. ("To" is used as a Preposition connecting the Noun "town" to the rest of the Sentence.)

In the case of the Infinitive, however, the word "to" is positioned in front of a Verb, and it will be called "the Infinitive Marker." It is easy to spot Infinitives because they will usually be preceded by "to" (to keep, to run, to jump, to inspire, to fight, to play, and so forth). That's the good news. But, whereas the Gerund can be used only as a Noun and the Participle can only be used as an Adjective—*the Infinitive can be used as a Noun, an Adjective, and even an Adverb.* Take a deep breath and proceed with a clear mind. You can handle this! Perhaps you will enjoy this final theme.

Heretofore, examples of Subjects have included only one word. "The *boy* hit the ball." With the coming of the Infinitive, that will change. There will be two words; one of them will always be the Infinitive Marker, "to."

Let's look at some Infinitives used as Nouns, in other words the Sentence Parts will be Subjects, Direct Objects, Indirect Objects, and Objects of Prepositions.

### Infinitives used as Nouns

1. *To go* was the best thing for Jed. "To go" is an Infinitive.

   "To go" is the Subject of the Sentence. The Infinitive "to go" is used as a Noun.

2. *To run* was a poor option for the thief. "To run" is an Infinitive.

   "To run" is the Subject of the Sentence. The Infinitive "to run" is used as a Noun.

3. He tried *to run* but was recaptured.

   "To run" is an Infinitive. "To run" is the Direct Object. He tried what? He tried to run. The Infinitive "to run" is used as a Noun.

4. The senator hoped *to carry* Alabama.

   "To carry" is an Infinitive. "To carry" is the Direct Object. The senator hoped what? He hoped to carry. The Infinitive "to carry" is used as a Noun.

Let's review: Nouns (from the raw material pile) can become Subjects, Direct Objects, Indirect Objects and Objects of the Preposition. Infinitives, since they can be used as Nouns, can also become Subjects, Direct Objects, Indirect Objects and Objects of the Preposition.

Infinitives may also be used as Adjectives (describing Nouns and telling which one, what kind, or how many).

### Infinitives used as Adjectives

1. He is the man *to elect*.

   "To elect" tells "which one" and describes the Noun "man." "To elect" is an Infinitive used as Adjective.

2. Jim's Café is the place *to eat*.

"To eat" tells "which one" and describes the Noun "place." "To eat" is an Infinitive used as an Adjective.

Infinitives may also be used as Adverbs, which describe Verbs and tell how, when, or where.

### Infinitives used as Adverbs

1. Jack strained *to jump* the bar.

   "To jump" describes (modifies) the Verb "strained." "To jump" is an Infinitive used as an Adverb.

2. He jogged *to keep* in shape.

   "To keep" describes (modifies) the Verb "jogged." "To keep" is an Infinitive used as an Adverb.

3. He worked *to defeat* poverty.

   "To defeat" describes (modifies) the Verb "worked." "To defeat" is an Infinitive used as an Adverb.

4. She sang *to inspire* the crowd.

   "To inspire" describes (modifies) the Verb "sang." "To inspire" is an Infinitive used as an Adverb.

Have you heard of the term "split infinitive"? This is a frequent error in exposition. However, since you know what an Infinitive is (Verb form introduced by "to"), this will be easy for you. *When you insert another word between the Infinitive marker "to" and the Verb, you have split it.* Let's look at some examples:

### Split Infinitives

1. Dad said to never give up. The Infinitive is "to give." See the splitting word, "never"?
2. Sally tried to always look neat. The Infinitive is "to look." See the splitting word, "always"?
3. It is a temptation to just get lazy. The Infinitive is "to get." See the splitting word, "just"?
4. He decided to aggressively pursue litigation. The Infinitive is "to pursue." See the splitting word, "aggressively"?
5. The professor wanted to better prepare his students for the future. The Infinitive is "to prepare." See the splitting word "better"? Sure you do. Good job!

6. I want to properly present Senator Jones. The Infinitive is "to present." See the splitting word "properly"?
7. The Texans were determined to courageously defend the Alamo. The Infinitive is "to defend." See the splitting word, "courageously"?

Now, how do you correct these Sentences? Simply move the splitting word to another part of the Sentence.

"I want to present Senator Jones *properly*."

"The Texans were determined to defend the Alamo courageously."

Keep your eye open for *Split Infinitives*. They can rear their ugly heads at every level of exposition in every type of document.

This is a bit beyond the scope of the handbook, but while we are in the neighborhood, let's learn it. It's gravy. Whoops! The author is back on the gustatory kick. Since Infinitives are part Verb, they can have Direct Objects.

Example: The soldiers struggled to carry the water.

Objects of Infinitives are as simple to find as Direct Objects of Verbs. In this case, find the Infinitive and ask what or whom. "To carry" what? And you have an answer, "water." It is the Object of an Infinitive.

Infinitives may also have Subjects.

Example: The CEO asked John to preside.

See how John is the Subject of the Infinitive "to preside"? Here comes a wrinkle. When the Subject of the Infinitive is a Pronoun, that Pronoun requires the Objective Case. Up until now, all Pronouns used as Subjects went in the Nominative Case. In the situation of the Subject of an Infinitive, this is no longer true.

Example: The chairman asked who/whom to serve as Chaplain?

The Pronoun (who/whom) is used as the Subject of the Infinitive "to serve." Subjects of Infinitives require the Objective Case; hence, "whom" is correct.

It is strange to say, "Subjects of Infinitives require the Objective Case," but it is a fact.

# Potpourri

There are many grammatical issues which did not surface during our brief journey through *Proper Form, Pure and Simple*. I shall briefly discuss some of these issues because they will be of great help to you. Students often remark that they learned more in Potpourri than in any other section. That, of course, is because the learners acquired a background during the journey through Proper Form that made the Potpourri section a sweet-smelling aroma to them. Although exceptions abound in our language, and the dynamic of English will produce even more, here are some basic guidelines that should serve you well in discovering the existing norm.

| 1. Unneeded words: | Incorrect | Correct |
|---|---|---|
| | I have "got" a headache. | I have a headache. |
| | I have "got" to do well. | I have to do well. |
| | Where is he "at"? | Where is he? |
| | Where did Jim go "to"? | Where did Jim go? |
| | Let's continue "on." | Let's continue. |

2. Effect/Affect:     Probably 95 percent of the time, *effect* will be a Noun—*affect* will be a Verb. The Noun "effect" means the result of something. The Verb "affect" means to change.

The *effect* (result) of the medicine is that it *affects* (changes) one's vision.

3. Farther/Further:     Farther = physical distance. Jim lives five miles *farther* down the road.

Further = degree (non-physical distance). I will discuss it no *further*.

These Adverbs (or Adjectives) are compared as follows:

Positive = far. Comparative = farther. Superlative = farthest. It was the farthest (physically distant) city from New York.

Positive = far. Comparative = Further. Superlative = Furthest. It was the furthest (non-physical distance) thought from my mind.

4. Between/Among:

Between = comparing two entities. The game was *between* the Lions and the Tigers.

Among = comparing three or more entities. The culinary contest was *among* the seven restaurants.

What's wrong with this Sentence? We had five good applicants; it was hard to choose between them. You are correct! It should have read, "It was hard to choose *among* them."

5. As/Than:    Supply the missing Verb principle

You are as tall as he/him.    Supply the missing Verb "is."

You are as tall as he (is tall).    *He* is correct.

Susan likes Jim more than I/me.    Supply the missing Verb "likes."

Susan likes Jim more than (she likes) me.    *Me* is correct.

6. Definite Article: The

Indefinite Article: A/An

Use "An" before words beginning with a vowel (A,E,I,O,U, or a vowel sound), except words beginning with a long "U" sound.

Examples: an apple, an essay, an igloo, an owl, an umbrella

Use "A" before words beginning with a consonant (letters other than vowels).

Examples: a bat, a chicken, a car, a clarinet, a tornado

A young lady, for whom English was her second language, wrote in her essay, "I attend an university in Oklahoma." I quickly circled the "an" as being incorrect. After class, she asked, "Aren't you supposed to use 'an' before words before beginning with a Vowel?" The answer was yes. "Isn't 'U' a Vowel?" The answer was yes. "Why is it wrong?" I had failed to teach her the second part of the rule, "except words beginning with a long 'U' sound." Words beginning with a long "U" sound should be preceded by the Indefinite Article "A." Here are some examples of the long "U" sound: a university, a utilitarian philosophy, a ubiquitous sound, a ukulele, a union.

Here is another wrinkle. Why is it correct to say, "an MBA Degree," when "M" is not a vowel? It is because of the unwritten vowel sound (E) MBA. You do the same for "an RCA Television," because of the unwritten vowel sound (A)RCA. In other words, use "An" before words that begin with a Vowel, whether that Vowel is written or sounded. Before going further into the discussion of "A" versus "An," let's restate the rule in order to get our bearings.

*Use "An" before words that begin with a vowel (A,E,I,O,U) whether written or sounded, except those beginning with a long 'U' sound."*

Take the word "honor." Although "H" is not a Vowel, the first sound you hear is a Vowel sound, "onor." The word "Honor" in a sense begins with the Vowel, "O." Hence, "It is *an* honor," is correct. The same is true for the word "Hour." The first sound you hear is "our," a vowel sound. Hence, "It has been *an* hour," is correct. You are in the same boat when you use the word "Honest." The first sound you hear is a vowel sound, "on-est." Hence, "Jim is *an* honest man," is correct. When the "H" is sounded, however, you retreat to the rule of using the Indefinite Article "A" before words that begin with a consonant (letters other than vowels). Since "H" is a consonant and not a vowel, we must use the Indefinite Article "A" before words beginning with the sounded "H." "Jack is *a* humble man," would be correct. "The bird was *a* hawk," would be correct. It was *a* harvest moon. It was *a* heartfelt tribute.

Another "H" word that causes debate is the word "historic." Since "H" is a Consonant and not a Vowel, we must use the Indefinite Article "A" before it. Older scholars get up in arms here. They will say and will write, "This is an historic occasion." Possibly this is a throwback to the

British and their refusal to sound the "H." In effect, they are sounding the Sentence this way, "This is an 'istoric' occasion," in which case "an" would be correct because the first sound you hear is the Vowel sound "I." (If at a croquet game in London, you would hear, "Well it! Well it!") To be honest, there is trend toward accepting both "an historic occasion" and "a historic occasion" as being correct. But you know the rule, "a historic occasion," is your answer.

7. Principal/Principle:   Principal: From the Latin word for "chief"; chief teacher, major element

"The *principal* of Hoover Elementary is Clyde Smith."

Principle = idea, tenet, or rule.

"The *principle* of honesty is at stake."

8. Ensure/Insure:   Ensure = guarantee

"The faculty works hard to ensure that students are well educated."

Insure = pay premiums

"My brother works nights to insure his new car."

9. Capital/Capitol:   Capital = From the Latin word for "head"; head money, head city, head letter

"Clyde worked hard to secure capital for his business."

Capitol = physical location of seat of government—the building.

"Caesar built a new Capitol on the Capitoline hill near Rome."

10. Maybe/May be:   Maybe = perhaps, possibly

"Maybe I'll go home."

May be = perchance, might be, could be.

"Jim *may be* the next governor."

11. All right/ Alright    All right = safe, accurate

"We are all right." "The balance sheets were all right."

Alright = after all.

"Santa Claus came to our house, alright."

(Alright is not accepted as a word by some scholars. However, it keeps trying to enter the language with a degree of dignity carrying the connotation of "after all.")

12. All ready/ Already    All ready = prepared.

"We are all ready."

Already = beforehand.

"Already, his feet were frozen."

13. Imply/Infer    Imply = hint

"Did you imply that he was overpaid?"

Infer = conclude.

"You may infer that the company is in the black based on these financials."

14. Double negative: It is incorrect to use two words meaning "no" in the same Sentence.

| Incorrect: | Correct: |
|---|---|
| I can't hardly wait. | I can hardly wait. |
| I don't have nothing. | I don't have anything. |
| I scarcely need no clothes. | I scarcely need any clothes. |

15. Subject/Verb Agreement: When there are two Subjects

Neither the players nor the coach know/*knows* for sure.

Coach = singular; (he) knows. Make the Verb agree with the Subject in the Sentence that is closer to the Verb.

Neither the coach nor the players *know*/knows for sure.

Players = plural; (they) know.

16. Numbers: There are many rules and regulations involving numbers. In some manuals of style, you spell out the numbers one to ten. Of course, if you are giving the score of a baseball game, it would be "11 to 9" as opposed to "11 to nine." In other manuals, you would spell out the numbers one to one hundred. Different disciplines require specialized treatment of numbers.

17. Hyphens: There are also many guidelines for hyphens. It is difficult to find a hard and fast rule that applies in every case. Your dictionary or style guide will be your best resource. Here are some generally accepted guidelines regarding the use of the hyphen.

    Hyphenate numbers twenty-one through ninety-nine.

    "*Fifty-five* men served on the task force."

    Hyphenate compound (two part) Adjectives used before a Noun.

    "Shakespeare is a *well-known* author."

    "The Baker Company and Well's advertising have a *long-term* agreement."

18. Redundancy: This word means saying the same thing twice. Re: is a Latin word meaning, "again."

Here are some examples: repeat again, refer back, alternative choice, armed gunman, attach together, merge together, marry with, continue on, ascend up, descend down, unite as one, explode out, divide in two, progress forward, digress back, open up, close down, and so forth. The literal meaning of redundant is to "overflow again." Many errors of redundancy occur when a Latin prefix is used and an English word is added. The Latin Preposition "ex" used as a prefix means "out." When you write "explode out" you have said "out" twice; once with the Latin prefix "ex" and once with the English word "out." The same holds true for many common redundancies; for example "di" means "two," "re" means "again or back," and "pro" means "forward." So when you say "divide in two," "repeat again," and "progress forward," you have been redundant because you have said the same thing twice.

20. It's versus Its: "It's" is a contraction meaning, "it is."

> "*It's* a beautiful day in the neighborhood."

> "Its" is a Possessive Pronoun.

> "The cardinal raised *its* beautiful red head."

21. Two = The number. "*Two* roads diverged in a yellow wood."

To = The Preposition (and/or the Infinitive marker) "I am going *to* town." "*To* go would be fun."

Too = Also. "Clyde wanted to invest in the IPO, *too.*"

22. Accept/Except:    Accept = to receive.

> "Will you *accept* the invitation to be the keynote speaker?"

> Except = to leave out (usually a Preposition).

> "All were present at the retreat *except* Vice President Jones."

> Except as a Verb:

"The President *excepted* (left out) the tardy workers from the bonus plan."

23. Some time = a period of time. "You will need *some time* to study."

Sometime = an unspecified time. "*Sometime* in the future, gasoline will be cheap."

Sometimes = occasionally. "*Sometimes*, I need extra energy."

24. Lose = to fail. "It's no fun to *lose.*"

Loose = not restrained. "Help! The trailer is *loose!*" "*Loose* lips sink ships."

25. Patients = any recipient of medical attention, care, or treatment. "Dr. Jones had many *patients* yesterday."

Patience = to endure without complaint. "Job had great *patience.*"

26. Here = in this place. "We are *here* to honor the Chairman of the Board."

Hear = auditory response. "Do you *hear* me now?"

27. Sell = to cause to take. "Did you *sell* your *house*?"

Sale = offering of goods. "Was the dress on sale?"

28. Counsel = advice, especially legal advice. "Did you receive wise *counsel* from your attorney?"

Council = assembly of officials. "The city *council* will meet on Tuesday."

29. Illicit = not allowed by law or custom. "It was an *illicit* relationship."

Elicit = to draw out. "Did the President *elicit* loud applause?"

30. There = in that place. "*There* he is, behind the fence."

They're = contraction, meaning, "They are." "*They're* coming to town tomorrow."

Their = Possessive Pronoun. "*Their* costumes were beautiful."

Congratulations. Bring out the turkey, cornbread dressing, giblet gravy, and the cranberry sauce with the pecans and marshmallows in it! You have hung in there throughout *Proper Form, Pure and Simple*. To many of you, this journey has served as a reemphasis of principles which were swimming in your head (knowledge), but had never been categorized (understanding). To others, the majority of the concepts were brand new. Regardless of the group you represent, it is now time to take your knowledge, and understanding, and apply them to real-life situations (wisdom).

I wish I could have looked into your face and answered your questions. It would have been good to have known you personally. However, the fact that you chose to improve yourself by studying these fundamental principles speaks volumes about you. You, as a career learner, are no doubt bright and full of potential and are able to entertain the idea of further studies in Proper Form and any other discipline that delights you. Face the future with feet flat on the floor and confidence in your heart that you can write and speak in Proper Form. Godspeed!

# Bibliography

Axelrod, Rise B. and Charles R. Cooper. *The St. Martin's Guide to Writing*. 7th ed. Boston: Bedford/St. Martin's, 2004.

Chandler, Francis. *Fundamentals of Business Communication*. Chicago: Irwin, 1995.

Curme, George O. *English Grammar*. New York: Barnes & Noble, 1947.

Enos, Theresa, ed. *Encyclopedia of Rhetoric and Composition*. New York: Routledge, 1996.

Fowler, H. Ramsey and Jane E. Aaron, *The Little, Brown Handbook*. 4th ed. Glenview, IL: Scott, Foresman, 1989.

Hacker, Diana. *A Writer's Reference*. 5th ed. Boston: Bedford/St. Martin's, 2003.

Jenney, Charles Jr. *Second Year Latin*. Boston: Allyn and Bacon, 1954.

Lunsford, Andrea A. *The Everyday Writer,* 3rd ed. Boston: Bedford/St. Martin's, 2005.

Maxwell, John C. *The 21 Irrefutable Laws of Leadership*. Nashville: Nelson, 1998.

McWhorter, Kathleen. *Successful College Writing*. 2nd ed. Boston: Bedford/St. Martin's, 2003.

Scholes, Robert. *The Practice of Writing*. 5th ed. Boston: Bedford/St. Martin's, 2001.

Shertzer, Margaret. *The Elements of Grammar*. New York: Macmillan, 1986.

Smith, C. Alphonso. *Our Language*. Atlanta: Johnson, 1903.

Stoddard, Alexander and Matilda Bailey, *English, Fourth Course*. New York: American Books, 1951.

Timm, Paul R. *Basic Business English and Communication*. Englewood Cliffs, NJ: Prentice-Hall, 1986.

Watkins, Floyd C. *Practical English Handbook*. Boston: Houghton Mifflin, 1974.

West, Rinda. *Myself Among Others*. Glenview, IL: Scott, Foresman, 1990.

Whitlock, David Wesley. *Opportunity*. Eugene, OR: Wipf & Stock, 2007.